J. E. Clemson

B.A., DIP.ED., DIP.R.ED.

formerly Head of R.E. Department,
Servite Convent, Brown's Town, Jamaica

with advice from
MURIEL LYNCH

Chairman, Religious Education Sub-committee,
Ministry of Education, Jamaica

Nelson

Thomas Nelson & Sons Ltd
Lincoln Way, Windmill Road,
Sunbury-on-Thames, Middlesex TW16 7HP
P.O. Box 73146 Nairobi, Kenya
77 Coffee Street, San Fernando, Trinidad

Thomas Nelson (Australia) Ltd
19-39 Jeffcott Street, West Melbourne, Victoria 3003

Thomas Nelson and Sons (Canada) Ltd
81 Curlew Drive, Don Mills, Ontario

Thomas Nelson (Nigeria) Ltd
8 Ilupeju Bypass, PMB 1303 Ikeja, Lagos

First published 1974
Reprinted 1975, 1976
ISBN 0 17 566068 9

Biblical illustrations by the
Benedictine nuns of Cockfosters.
Other illustrations by Sarah Hale

Printed photolitho in Great Britain by
Ebenezer Baylis and Son Limited,
The Trinity Press, Worcester, and London

Contents

Acknowledgements

The author acknowledges with gratitude the assistance of the following people with the preparation of this book: Members of the sub-committee of the R.E. Curriculum Committee which produced the syllabus; Miss M. Lynch, Headmistress, St Hilda's High School; Head Deaconess Cecil Bishop; The Rev J. Hosie, S.J., St George's College, Kingston; The Rev K. Webster, Excelsior School, Kingston; advice and encouragement from Rev Anthony Bullen, Christian Education Centre, Liverpool, England.

Headmistress, Staff and Pupils of the Servite Convent, Brown's Town, Mr S. E. Edmondson, R.E. Officer, Jamaica Ministry of Education, and all those, without whose faith, encouragement and inspiration this series would never have been produced.

The author and publishers also wish to thank the following for permission to use copyright material included in the book: Collins Publishers for New Testament extracts from GOOD NEWS FOR MODERN MAN © American Bible Society, New York 1966, 1971; Orlando Patterson for extract from THE VISITOR; Methodist Publishing House for extract from YOUR GOD IS TOO SMALL by J. B. Phillips; Old Testament extracts taken from the JERUSALEM BIBLE published and © 1966, 1967 and 1968 by Darton Longman & Todd Ltd and Doubleday & Co Inc and are used by permission of the publishers; Hamish Hamilton Ltd for *Suicide* by Judy Miles from BREAKLIGHT edited by Andrew Salkey; William Heinemann Ltd for extract from HERE WE GO ROUND THE MULBERRY BUSH by Hunter Davies; extract from THE DIARY OF ANNE FRANK by permission of the publishers Vallentine Mitchell, 67 Great Russell Street, London W.C.1; Macmillan, London and Basingstoke for extract from WHAT'S IT ALL ABOUT by Vadim Frolov; Lutterworth Press for prayers on pp. 26 & 98 from INTERROBANG by Norman Habel; Arthur James Ltd for extract from YOUTH TO THE RESCUE by Lawrence Bailey; Samuel Selvon for extract from CANE IS BITTER; *If it turns out* reprinted with permission from DON'T JUST STAND THERE! by Earnest Larsen, C.SS.R., a Liguorian Book, © 1969 Liguori

Publications, Liguori, Mo. 63057; *My Parents Kept Me from Children who were Rough* reprinted by permission of Faber and Faber Ltd from COLLECTED POEMS 1928–53 by Stephen Spender; The Clarendon Press for extracts from Alan T. Dale's NEW WORLD © 1967 Oxford University Press; Vance Packard and Longmans for extract from THE HIDDEN PERSUADERS by Vance Packard; extract from BREAK FOR COMMERCIALS by Edith Rudinger and Vic Kelly reprinted by permission of Penguin Books Ltd; Search Press Ltd for extract from GROWING TO MATURITY by Dorothy Berridge; Collins Publishers for extract from COME OUT THE WILDERNESS by Bruce Kenrick; extract from *Renascence* by Edna St Vincent Millay from COLLECTED POEMS, Harper & Row © 1917, 1945 by Edna St Vincent Millay; Shada Music for *I'd Like to Teach the World to Sing*; *Freedom Come, Freedom Go* (R. Cook/R. Greenaway/Hammond Hazlewood) © 1971 for the World by Cookaway Music Ltd/A.I.R. Overworld Music Ltd; Mrs Sonia Brownwell Orwell and Secker & Warburg for extract from *1984*; Jonathan Cape Ltd for extract from DARKNESS AT NOON by Arthur Koestler.

Thanks are also due to the following for the use of photographs: Barnaby's Picture Library, p. 64(2); Cyril Bernard, p. 31; Anne Bolt, pp. 35, 47, 49(top), 56, 58, 121; Craig Burleigh, pp. 3, 14, 60, 103; Camera Press, pp. 11, 12, 37(photo: Stuart Heydinger), 43, 67(photo: Alan Clifton), 110(photo: Paul Almasy), 127; J. Allan Cash, pp. 17, 77, 84; Centre for Religious Education, Kingston, pp. x, 30; Currys Ltd, p. 88; Gleaner Photo, pp. 69(2), 87; Inter-Varsity Fellowship of Evangelical Unions, p. 114; Israel Government Tourist Office, p. 65; Jamaica Information Service, p. 95(bottom); Jamaica Tourist Board, p. 55; M.G.M., p. 90; Marvel Comics, p. 93; Methodist Missionary Society, p. 96; Nuggets for the Needy, pp. 71, 72; Bristol-Myers, p. 86; Shell Trinidad Ltd, p. 48; U.S.P.G., pp. 10, 45, 49(bottom), 57.

The publishers have made every effort to make the list of acknowledgements complete, but in some cases all efforts to trace the owners of the copyright failed. It is hoped that any such omissions will be excused.

To the Teacher

This series of textbooks is designed for the student, to stimulate thought and discussion on a personal level about many aspects of life in relation to religion. The themes explored in the third book are those selected for Grade 9 in the interdenominational Religious Education syllabus of the Jamaican Ministry of Education.

The approach used in the series may be novel to many teachers. Although the Bible is central to the study of Christianity, which is the main concern of the syllabus, it is not presented in the chronological fashion that has been the accepted method of introducing young people to Christianity. Instead, by concentrating on the young students in their community, it is hoped that they will be able to discover for themselves the constant loving activity of God in Creation and in all human life, in bringing all things to full maturity and glory in Christ his Son.

The material provided for each theme should give the student some insight into human experience, explored in relation to human and religious values. It is suggested that teachers who have time and opportunity should use other material in the syllabus to provide further guidelines and information as and when appropriate for their own class.

The aim of the series is not to provide a complete religious education for all students, of all denominations. This is clearly the task of leaders and families within each religious group. However, used with imagination and understanding it should enable Christians and non-Christians to reflect together on their experience and the experience of others in seeking truth and goodness in life, to train them to share their ideas with tolerance and understanding of the other person's point of view, and to enable them to develop a positive attitude towards their own potential as human beings in their own communities.

Education in general is benefiting from new insights into the psychological and social developments of children and adolescents. New methods and materials are being introduced in all subject areas. Religious Education is vitally important in the total personal development of the student and can benefit, with other subjects, in adopting new approaches that can maintain interest and involvement and, above all, deepen the sense of personal value and dignity that grows as we realise that we are born for a new life, given to us by Christ.

'I am come that you may have life and have it more abundantly,' (John 10, v. 10).

J. E. CLEMSON

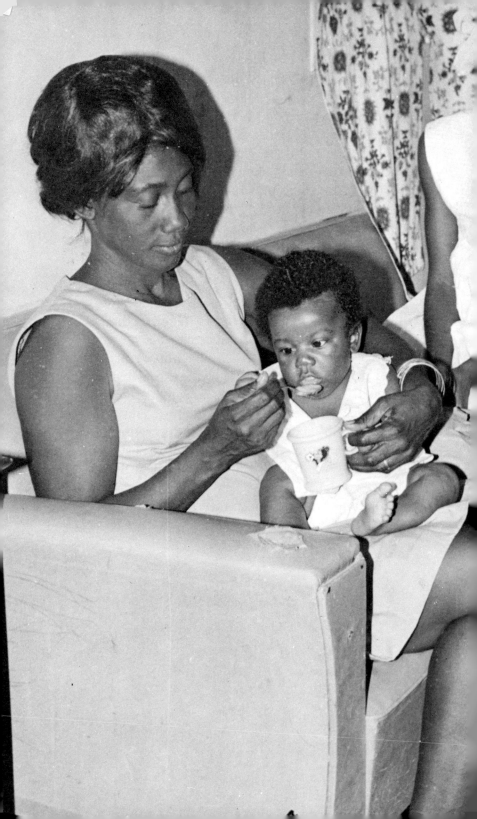

1 Family and friends

A new baby is a great joy for Mr and Mrs Jones. They have been planning for his arrival, and have every hope of providing a safe and happy home for him.

A new baby for Mrs Smith is a real problem. She already has seven children, and a poor home. There is no man in the house, yet her children are happy.

These children will be happy because they are loved and wanted. Then, although they may not have the best clothes, food, or homes, they will be important as people in their families.

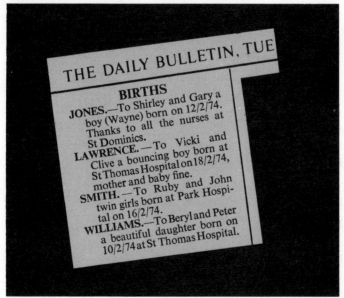

THE DAILY BULLETIN, TUE

BIRTHS

JONES.—To Shirley and Gary a boy (Wayne) born on 12/2/74. Thanks to all the nurses at St Dominics.

LAWRENCE.—To Vicki and Clive a bouncing boy born at St Thomas Hospital on 18/2/74, mother and baby fine.

SMITH.—To Ruby and John twin girls born at Park Hospital on 16/2/74.

WILLIAMS.—To Beryl and Peter a beautiful daughter born on 10/2/74 at St Thomas Hospital.

Most people find a place for themselves, and a future in their community, through the family to which they belong. You and your friends were born and have started your lives in a small group of people who are bound together and depend on one another because of a blood relationship. A man and a woman have given life to another human being. The mystery of why each of us is born at a certain place, of certain parents, and what our lives are to be, is known only to God our Father, who has given us the gift of life in this particular group at a special time in history. The boy or girl is usually grateful for the gift of life and for the care that is necessary to make him or her grow and develop properly. This is a longer period than for most other living creatures and is one reason why family life is so important.

Age at which:

	Kitten	Calf	Human child	Kid
Feeds itself				
Walks				
Communicates				

Can you fill in the details?

Write a short account of the ways in which a human child depends on its parents. Explain how it gradually becomes independent.

Most communities give an important place to parents. A society can be called 'patriarchal', because the father has the greater amount of influence, or 'matriarchal', because the mother

Facing the future as friends

has more power. Which do you think is true of your country? Or are men and women both valued equally and taking a fair share of the responsibility?

Sharon Smith is fourteen years old and takes no notice when her mother asks her to be in by ten o'clock. She will not say with whom she is spending time. There is a lot of talk in the town about the rough behaviour of gangs of teenagers and Mr Smith is afraid his daughter may get involved.

You may know parents of boys and girls who are having this kind of difficulty.

Do you think that most help is needed by the parents or by the teenagers? What will you do to avoid such situations when you become a parent?

Good parents are expected to train their children to take a proper place in the community. They are not always successful and there are often tragedies when young people reject their parents, leave home, or take up a way of life that causes them distress and shame.

Some parents, of course, feel that their children are always their 'children'. They do not allow them to grow up and live their own lives. These parents usually find that their children can be rebellious and resentful, and bring them trouble.

As in any other relationship, mutual trust has to allow differences of opinion and temperament, and real freedom of action.

Most boys and girls realise that their parents want them to be happy and set them high standards. They know that their parents have problems and difficulties. There has to be understanding on both sides. St Paul knew what the problem could be. Can you see that it would improve things if people tried to understand and live in God's way? Do things go wrong so often in families which go to church regularly?

Even this may not be a help. Members of a family must trust one another and help each other if things go wrong. This is really the best way of showing that Christ's love does mean something in a family and that each member is not only free to do what they believe is right, but can learn to act responsibly, with consideration for others.

Children, it is your Christian duty to obey your parents, for this is the right thing to do. 'Honour your father and mother' is the first commandment that has a promise added: 'so that all may be well with you, and you may live a long time in the land.'

Parents, do not treat your children in such a way as to make them angry. Instead, raise them with Christian discipline and instruction.

Ephesians 6, v. 1–4

Mothers and fathers are usually seen to have a definite role in family life. The mother is expected to care personally for the children, providing food, clothing and comfort when ill or in trouble. The father is expected to take the responsibility of providing the home, and the money to buy food and clothes. He usually has to make the final decision in family matters and act with authority.

However, there are very few families anywhere in the world where this pattern is true in every detail. In fact, it is probably closer to the truth to say that parents often share the responsibility of building a home and a family. A mother may earn money to help keep the family, and the father may help with the children. Other members of the family will also share the responsibilities.

Make a list of all the tasks that can be shared in the family. Why do many men feel that they should not take responsibility for bringing up their children? Why do women sometimes leave their children alone and uncared for? It is just laziness? Does such an attitude mean that they should not really have children?

Some modern doctors believe it is very important that children should have secure backgrounds, knowing that their parents really love them. Without this security, children can grow up as unhappy, frustrated persons if they feel that no one cares about them. If there is an unhappy background, faith in Jesus can help.

Lord Jesus, no-one cares. My mother left home and I have to look after myself. At school, I don't want to work and I'm always in trouble. Help me to face up to my feelings. I know you respect me and love me; help me to trust people who try to give me confidence and learn to share my life with others.   Amen

The following extract is part of a story. Read it, and answer the questions. It may help to deepen your understanding of the relationships within the family. The story is about a boy who has never known his father until he pays an unexpected visit.

I suppose she could be said to have been warm in her own way. But, unconsciously, she taught me not to expect very much and so I asked for very little. All I desired was for her to be there, always there. Now there was the threat of her departure.

But that was not possible. I reassured myself that I was being silly to the point of deciding that it would have been better if I left the room. Perhaps they wished to say adult things. As soon as I began to nudge my way to the door I heard him saying, in a manner which suggested that he was repeating himself, 'Yes, it's been a long time, Gladys'. I decided then that I was certainly the reason for their apparent discomfort, and I began to move less imperceptibly to the door. Suddenly I heard my mother call my name. Her voice was sharp and severe; she did not have to say that I must stay; her tone was enough.

The stranger looked at me quizzically, then back at her, and suddenly sprang out of his chair. He made the usual motions which indicated an intention to depart; yet, he hesitated. Then he suddenly seemed to remember something. He took out a fifty-cent note from his trouser pocket and handed it to me.

'Buy a present with it,' he said.

I stared at the note, a little shocked, both at the large sum of money and at the fact that he, of all people, should have given it to me. I looked up at my mother to see what her response was. I was not surprised when she said, 'Give it back'. Then she turned to him and said, 'I bring 'im up all this time without your help; I don't need it now'.

I immediately held the money out to him for I realised that my mother was in no mood to be crossed. I began to dread the moment when I would be alone with her.

The man began to protest, but he broke off suddenly and took back the note from me. I began to feel sorry for him, for he seemed insulted and sad. He took up his little felt hat, put it on his head, and left without saying another word. I never saw him again.

Orlando Patterson

1 Security means feeling safe. Do you think the boy has enough security? Is it possible to feel safe if you know someone loves you even if they are not there with you all the time?

2 'But unconsciously, she taught me not to expect very much and so I asked for very little'.

Do you think the boy would have been taught to expect more if his father had been with the family?

3 Do you think the mother should have told the boy to give back the fifty-cent note? Would you have liked to think the boy would see him again?

4 Do you think the father and mother really loved one another or intended to marry?

5 What difference would it have made to the story

if the mother had been more forgiving and the father had been more understanding of the mother's feelings?

6 Why do you think the father came to visit? Is a son important to his father?

7 What would Jesus have said about the situation?

8 Read the story of the Prodigal Son. This story reminds us how God forgives us and expects us to forgive others. Why is it so difficult for the mother to forgive the man in the story?

Ideally, family life is the basis for growing up happily so that you move out to share the life of the wider community, with confidence. Eventually, you leave home and build a life of your own. The image of God as a Father in the story of the Prodigal Son, for it has a deeper spiritual meaning, is only one occasion when Jesus emphasised that we belong to another family within which we develop, grow, and move on. If we can accept the idea of the family of God, to which everyone belongs, then our destiny is to share our lives with others, even though this seems almost impossible in practice.

It is easy to mix with people like ourselves. We judge people by their clothes, their voices, and their possessions. But we can be caught out by this superficial way of valuing them, for we may not be able to trust them. It is more difficult to be interested in people whose way of life seems wrong or strange to us. If people are ill or in trouble, it is easy to hand out money or gifts. But does this help to change the conditions that cause unhappiness, or to restore self-respect? A breakdown in love and trust in a family will affect the rest of the community. An abandoned child, a teenager in trouble, an old person who needs too much attention, must have care in the wider community if the family has failed. There are two kinds of people, and perhaps many of us are a mixture of both.

God is always ready to help you try again

Old people are the responsibility of us all

Compare these two versions of the Beatitudes. It is quite obvious that the people who are living to the standard set by Jesus are needed to heal the suffering caused by those in the second group.

Group I

Happy are those who know they are spiritually poor;
    the Kingdom of heaven belongs to them!
Happy are those who mourn;
    God will comfort them!
Happy are the meek;
    they will receive what God has promised!
Happy are those whose greatest desire is to do
    what God requires;
    God will satisfy them fully!
Happy are those who are merciful to others;
    God will be merciful to them!
Happy are the pure in heart;
    they will see God!
Happy are those who work for peace among men;
    God will call them his sons!
Happy are those who are persecuted because they
    do what God requires:
    the Kingdom of heaven belongs to them!

Matthew 5, v. 3–10

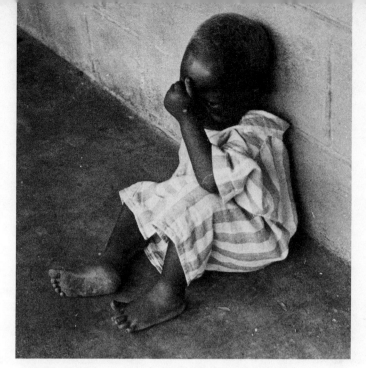

Is there no one to care for this abandoned child?

Here is an extract from J. B. Phillips' *Your God is Too Small*:

Group II

Happy are the pushers;
    for they get on in the world.
Happy are the hard-boiled;
    for they never let life hurt them.
Happy are they who complain;
    for they get their own way in the end.
Happy are the blasé;
    for they never worry over their sins.
Happy are the slave-drivers;
    for they get results.
Happy are the knowledgeable men of the world;
    for they know their way around.
Happy are the troublemakers;
    for people have to take notice of them.

Has this girl's family failed her?

We know from the life of Jesus that it is central to his mission to help people everywhere, of all time, to realise that life may become really worthwhile only if it is lived in a spirit of love.

This heals the torment of the struggle within ourselves, builds a peaceful community with others and unites us, above all, to God who is our Father.

He emphasised how much our lives are interrelated with God and other people, by summing up the purpose of life as follows:

A certain teacher of the Law came up and tried to trap Jesus. 'Teacher', he asked, 'what must I do to receive eternal life?'

Jesus answered him, 'What do the Scriptures say? How do you interpret them?'

The man answered, ' "You must love the Lord your God with all your heart, with all your soul, with all your strength, and with all your mind"; and, "You must love your fellow-man as yourself." '

'Your answer is correct', replied Jesus, 'do this and you will live'.

Luke 10, v. 25–28

It is a constantly fascinating mystery to study the truth of this statement. We cannot carry out one part of this commandment without involving the other two parts.

We need love like plants need light. Unless we have a positive loving attitude to ourselves, we cannot love others. Unless we love others, we cannot love God who is love. Neglect of one part of the commandment will affect the way we live according to the other.

> We love because God first loved us. If someone says, 'I love God,' but hates his brother, he is a liar. For he cannot love God, whom he has not seen, if he does not love his brother, whom he has seen. This, then, is the command that Christ gave us: he who loves God must love his brother also.
>
> 1 John 4, v. 19–21

In family life one experiences all the tensions of having to live in a close relationship with others, whom you may not even like very much. Often the very closeness of the family tie can create bitterness and dislike over matters that are quite trivial. Members of a family do not get on with each other automatically – there may be bitter quarrels.

Mary heard that her sister had criticised a dress

she had bought. She refused to speak to her afterwards, even though her sister apologised. They did not become friends again until ten years later when their mother died.

Make a list of reasons why members of families usually quarrel. Is it always easy to make up afterwards? Why is it that sometimes two members of a family do not speak to each other for twenty years?

People often look for real friendship, where they can share their lives in trust and confidence with someone else, outside the family circle. Most people have friends, but sometimes take them too much for granted.

Do her friends really care?

The following poem is about someone who did not have a friend when he needed one. It makes clear that the responsibility we have for the lives of others is quite terrifying.

Suicide

Memory searches
the sea of the mind
until, at last, a barb of guilt
Harpoons those hours
to his face.

For when his heart
driven before a gale
Of loneliness
Sought in our hearts
a harbour and a home
No sigh we gave
To anchor our compassion
in his soul.

Not silence itself was our sin
for touching hands
turn silence to a delicate
exquisite thing, slender
breath of a dawn camp fire
on this beach and eloquent
as a lone seagull's flight;
Why is tenderness usually late
or, if it does come
frail as foam?

Judy Miles

On the next page are some quotations made by people through history about friendship. It may help you to assess your standards by these, and to discover where people need to develop their ideals a little.

A faithful friend is a strong defence: and he that hath found such a one hath found a treasure.

Ecclesiasticus 6, v. 14

But in deed
A friend is never known till a man have need.

John Heywood, 1497–1580

If you have a friend worth loving
Love him, Yes, and let him know
That you love him, ere life's evening
Tinge his brow with sunset glow.
Why should good words ne'er be said
Of a friend till he is dead.

Daniel Hoyt, 1845–1936

A friend is a person with whom I
may be sincere. Before him, I may
think aloud.

Emerson, 1803–1882

For how many things which for our sake
we should never do, do we perform for
the sake of our friends.

Cicero, 104–43 BC

He removes the greatest ornament of
friendship, who takes away from it respect.

Cicero

Sometimes we may demand too much from our friends. We expect them to satisfy our deep desire for completeness and harmony in ourselves and in life. Perhaps this is one reason why people who appear to be complete opposites form friendships. A pretty girl and a plain one; a lively person and a quiet one; a friendly person and a solitary one — these may seem odd partners. Can you see how, in fact, it could be a damaging kind of relationship

as well as a helpful one? It is possible to try to make up for your own deficiencies and weaknesses through your friendships, and it is also possible to use your friends to prove your own superiority. A plain girl may get more attention if she has an attractive girl friend, but is it the right kind of attention? It is a good idea to pray for guidance in friendships, for friends influence us in many ways that we do not realise until much later.

This is a prayer you could say – or make up a prayer of your own.

Lord, a real friend is someone who values you for yourself, accepts you for what you are and helps you to become the person you really can be. Help me to be honest with myself about my friends, so that I do not debase my ideals by trying to be popular, by making friends with people only because they are useful to me, by being ready to join in criticism of my friends if others do not approve of them. Remind me of the way you shared your life with your friends so that through my self-giving, others may learn to give in trust and love. Amen

What is love?
 Trusting?
  Sharing?
   Caring?
    Forever?
     Whatever happens?
      Self-giving so that the other person may be
      happy?

The following is a description of how a boy felt
when he met a girl for the first time. Do you think
that people really feel like this? Is it right to expect
so much from 'falling in love'?

'When shall we two meet again?' I said, putting on a
squeaky voice to cover up my nervousness. This
might be the end of a very short road.
 'How about tomorrow night?' I said.
 She couldn't but she made it the day after. She
smiled and my heart leapt.
 Mary went in and closed the door. I bounced
back down the road, killing myself laughing, singing
and shouting like mad, jumping around inside and
outside and all over the pavement. My heart was
dancing with the crescent moon. I felt light and
drunk. I wasn't worried about missing my bus home,
I'd rather walk anyway. I'd be alone, no buses, no
people, no noise, a long walk home. Mary and me,
me and Mary, would be together for ever.

Hunter Davies

It is true, though, that many people often see
that their only hope of achieving all the possibilities
that love seems to offer is to be found in the love
relationship between men and women.
 Even if they do not marry, people in love feel
that nothing can ever separate them, and that,

unless they can share their lives and find happiness together, life is not worth living. Many pop songs have this theme. Can you think of examples from past and present hit songs?

Finding out what love can mean causes all kinds of complications in life as people grow up. The first time people fall in love is often a very shattering experience. It can seem impossible that anyone else has ever felt as you do.

To speak of being 'in love', however, is to view love with another dimension – that of sexual attraction. Far too often we use the word 'love' in its deepest sense when the relationship may be a very superficial one, based on a physical feeling that may last only a few days or weeks.

Yet it is very important to understand the power and dignity and value of the physical sex relationship, which means a great deal to both men and women.

The word 'sex' has many shades of meaning.

It can be the section on the birth certificate where a new child is classified as male or female.

It can refer to the power of human beings to reproduce as a result of the joining of their bodies in sexual union. It can refer simply to the sex act — the physical act of union, which can bring great pleasure or pain to two people on various levels, physical, emotional, and spiritual.

It can mean the expression of love between two people, and is the only way in which they can express their desire for the closest possible union on every level as persons.

It is a word that seems to equal wrong doing in the minds of some people, who believe that there is nothing more terrible than sexual sin. Perhaps they are afraid of or disgusted by sex. This attitude makes it hard for them to forgive someone else or to forgive themselves for sexual misbehaviour. Sex is good unless used selfishly. As always, Jesus made it clear that mercy and forgiveness rather than harsh judgement and condemnation, are needed to face sinful situations. Read the story of the woman taken in adultery in St John's Gospel, chapter 8.

In the *Diary of Anne Frank* there is a description of her relationship with a boy called Peter, who shares her captivity. She experiences many of the strains and tensions felt by young people in their first love affair.

She looks forward to her first kiss:

Sunday morning, just before eleven o'clock,
16th April, 1944

Darlingest Kitty,

Remember yesterday's date, for it is a very important day in my life. Surely it is a great day for every girl when she receives her first kiss? Well, then, it is just as important for me, too! Bram's kiss on my right cheek doesn't count any more, likewise the one from Mr Walker on my right hand.

How did I suddenly come by this kiss? Well, I will tell you.

Yesterday evening at eight o'clock I was sitting with Peter on his divan. It wasn't long before his arm went round me. 'Let's move up a bit,' I said, 'then I don't bump my head against the cupboard.' He moved up, almost into the corner, I laid my arm under his and across his back, and he just about buried me, because his arm was hanging on my shoulder.

Now we've sat like this on other occasions, but never so close together as yesterday. He held me firmly against him, my left shoulder against his chest; already my heart began to beat faster, but we had not finished yet. He didn't rest until my head was on his shoulder and his against it. When I sat upright again after about five minutes, he soon took my head in his hands and laid it against him once more. Oh, it was so lovely, I couldn't talk much, the joy was too great. He stroked my cheek and arm a bit awkwardly, played with my curls and our heads lay touching most of the time. I can't tell you, Kitty, the feeling that ran through me all the while, I was too happy for words, and I believe he was as well.

It is very clear from this passage from Anne Frank's diary, how happy she felt in her relationship with Peter. But how would he have felt?

Boys are usually more easily aroused physically than girls, and more at the mercy of their desires if they experiment with sex. Because of this, they are seen as more likely to be selfish in their attitudes. But girls can be equally selfish if they want to claim a particular boy as their property. Both boys and girls have to face the question of whether they really care for the other as a person, or whether they are only interested in sex for its own sake.

The following extract is from a story about a Russian boy, called *What's it all about?* by Vadim Frolov. He has just kissed a girl, and is worried about how he should see the situation. He speaks to his father about it:

'Papa, how old were you when you started kissing girls?'

And I grabbed my head. What was I saying? What an ass I was! I'd wanted to talk about something entirely different, and suddenly look what I'd done!

My father grunted, and examined me closely. It was good that he didn't laugh; if he had so much as smiled, I would probably have sunk right into the ground.

'Well, go on, tell me about it,' my father said.

So I, as red as a boiled lobster and stuttering over every word, told him all about Lelka.

'Is that . . . very bad?' I asked at the end, panting. It was a silly question, but somehow I had to ask it.

My father stood up and now he began to walk up and down the room. 'Once you've told me about it, then . . . Listen, now . . . well, do you like her, or not?'

I shook my head. Here was what I had been thinking about, all along, only I couldn't puzzle it out for myself – the whole problem was just this: 'Do you like the girl or not? If you like her, there's no harm in kissing her, but if not, then something's

not right . . .' But what could I say about Lelka?
As a girl, she was – well, all right, pretty and had
the kind of figure girls ought to have, and of course
I'd have been lying if I'd said that I didn't like her at
all. But what wasn't right was that I liked her only
in one sense, well, as you like a pretty picture, or
something like that. When I don't see her, I don't
remember her at all – it's only right now that I can't
get her out of my head, and that's what annoys me.
But I think about Natasha all the time, and even
when I'm not thinking about her it's just as if I
were . . . I don't know how to say this, but it's the way
people write in books: 'She was always with him,
even if he did not see her and did not think of her' –
or something like that.

I didn't say all this to my father, but just shook
my head again.

'I don't understand,' he said, and grew angry.
'Now don't shuffle! If you like her, say so.'

'No,' I said, 'that is . . . I like her, but . . .'

'Aha, I understand,' my father said. 'Then that's
bad. You don't have to kiss everybody you like,
but . . .'

I started to choke. God knows what had made
me talk about this, when I had wanted to talk to
him about something entirely different. I'd made it
look as if I'd had nothing to do with it; after all,
Lelka had started it all. But of course I didn't say this:
I realised in time that this would be too shameful . . .

'And don't you dare say that it was she who . . .
kissed you. Some scoundrels behave like that: they
take advantage of a girl and then they boast about it
to everybody they meet, and if you tell them it's
disgraceful, then they change their tune and say
they were seduced by the girl, and they are really as
pure as . . . as . . .' For some reason my father got
very excited and he went on talking for a long time
about how there are such men and how they deceive
poor unhappy women, for whom one should feel
sorry; there are so many assorted goats wandering

around that there's no way for them to feel safe. He spoke so passionately and so convincingly that I began to feel like a goat from whom unhappy women had no chance to escape. Then I thought that he had gone too far, and as soon as I started thinking this my father suddenly stopped short, sat down in his chair and waved his hand.

'I say this,' he said, tired out, 'not about you, but in general. On the other hand, it may be useful to you in the future. Well, what are you going to do about it?'

'I'm not going to . . . to kiss her any more,' I blurted out.

'Why not?' my father asked, and he laughed. 'It's probably very pleasant, isn't it?'

'Pleasant! pleasant!' I yelled. 'I come to you like a human being, and you just preach to me about goats, and now you make fun of me! Of course it's pleasant. As if you didn't know.'

'Don't get angry,' my father said. 'I really am saying something that isn't necessary. You want advice from me, and, sorry, I just have no advice on this to give you. Behave the way your intelligence . . . and your heart . . . tell you to. You're not stupid, and I think you've got a heart, too.'

'Thanks,' I growled.

At this point he got annoyed too.

'What do you want, recipes from me on just how to handle every incident in your life?' he said angrily. 'Don't wait for them. Or do you want me to tell you that you're still too young to start kissing, and that you ought to worry about your studies? It's already happened, do you want to slobber about it all the rest of your life? That's not the way a man handles things. The only thing I can tell you is this: in any situation, in the most complicated situation, you've got to behave, first of all, like a man and not like an animal. And now if you're going to start wasting your time on a lot of random kissing, then . . .' He waved his hand, was quiet for a little, and then said in a low voice: 'You'll lose what's most important, or rather, you'll never find it.'

Discussion points

1 In the first extract, do you think the kiss meant as much to Peter as it did to Anne? Are boys usually as romantic as girls?

2 Does Peter have a responsibility in helping to decide how far their relationship should go?

3 In the second extract, do you agree with the father when he says, 'Do you like the girl or not? If you like her, there's no harm in kissing her, but if not, then something's not right'?

4 Why is the father worried that 'too much random kissing' will mean 'You'll lose what's most important, or rather, you'll never find it.'?

5 Would you discuss such matters with your parents?

6 Apart from talking about their activities and relationships with their friends, do you think that many young people are seriously trying to find real meaning for sex in their relationships with each other? Or are they looking for a good time and not too much responsibility?

Most boys and girls have to learn to say 'No' when they are under pressure to give themselves physically to someone else, and have to stand out against all kinds of emotional blackmail, like 'We'll never see each other again,' 'I thought you loved me' – and so on. Because of the excitement and the need to give, it can be difficult to remember that having sex is much more than a simple physical act. Two persons are involved with their hopes and feelings, and a third person can be created as a result of their action. Disappointment and heartbreak are as usual as ecstasy and happiness in a sex relationship, as the boy who said this prayer discovered:

I had always dreamed
that making love to a lovely girl
would be like
bouncing slowly from a diving board
and then floating slowly
through the gentle air
until my body was surrounded
by the swirling crystal waters.

But it wasn't like that at all.
Something went wrong, very wrong.

It took a long time
before we agreed to go all the way.
We said we loved each other
and wanted to show that love.

It took a long time
before we said yes.

Then suddenly it was over.
Just like that, it was over,
and we lay there
saying nothing.

I was spent
and she was almost crying.
It was no fun for her,
not really.

And now I hate myself.
It wasn't worth it
and I hate myself for it.

It didn't help us
to grow closer,
it didn't help at all.

In fact we're further apart.
We're like strangers.

Lord, when will I be ready
for that kind of loving?

When are two people ready for loving
so that what happens
doesn't hurt either person
but binds them both together
and gives them something meaningful?
When, Lord, when?

Interrobang

Young people sometimes condemn strict stand-ards of morality as unreasonable and denying people a chance of happiness. Sometimes, this may simply mean that they are expecting too much of a sex relationship as instant happiness and also undervaluing what it really means.

For a Christian, the ideal of marriage is based on the need for partnership between men and women that is secure and permanent. This can obviously mean better family life. It can also mean deeper personal happiness for two people, who have shared joys and hardships in love, and feel that love is forever for them. Sex in such a relationship is a sacred sign of the loving unity and mutual comfort that exists between the couple. Pre-marital sex can rarely be an experience of this depth — and yet many young people see this as a right and necessary thing.

Study these reasons for and against pre-marital sex and trial marriages. They may help you to understand the situation more clearly.

Reasons for	Reasons against
1 If two people really love each other, it cannot be wrong to have sex.	But love does not always last, and when the attraction dies one person will certainly be hurt.
2 It's a good idea to find out if you are good sexual partners before you marry.	Sexual adjustment takes years and never is certain to last. It is only one aspect of a relationship between a man and a woman and should not be over-stressed at the expense of other values.
3 Relationships with a lot of different people can help you make a final decision.	Stress and strain of too many relationships can make it difficult to settle down to a permanent one.
4 The couple need not have children, if they use contraceptives, and can have a full relationship without them.	It is always possible that a child may be conceived and this could lead to great unhappiness. Most normal couples want children and this usually deepens their love for one another.

In the Christian ideal sex is so closely linked with self-sacrificing love in the marriage relationship that St Paul saw in it a reflection of the love Jesus pours out for the Christian Church. He portrays Jesus as the bridegroom and the Church as the bride.

Husbands, love your wives in the same way that Christ loved the church and gave his life for it. He did this to dedicate the church to God, by his word, after making it clean by the washing in water, in order to present the church to himself, in all its beauty, pure and faultless, without spot or wrinkle, or any other imperfection. Men ought to love their wives just as they love their own bodies. A man who loves his wife loves himself. (No one ever hates his own body. Instead, he feeds it and takes care of it, just as Christ does the church; for we are members of his body.) As the scripture says, 'For this reason, a man will leave his father and mother, and unite with his wife, and the two will become one.'

Ephesians 5, v. 25—31

This comparison gives a deeper appreciation of what the sex relationship can mean. It also reminds us of the dignity of the human body, through which love can be so perfectly expressed. Can you think of ways in which men and women can cause misery through their beauty and strength if they do not respect each other?

In the past marriage has been regarded as a legal and social contract, perhaps more than as a personal and religious commitment. Properly arranged marriages could result in increase of wealth and property, or a rise in the social scale. Children had marriages arranged for them as soon as they were born, with suitable partners, for family reasons. These marriages could be reasonably successful, and parents now are still concerned that their children should marry people of good standing and reputation.

However, in this century, both men and women are demanding more freedom in choosing their life partners; more importance is being given to the personal feelings that they have for each other.

A happy family at home

Divorce is easier now than it was a hundred years ago. This is a help to some people who find that they have made a wrong choice — but perhaps it would be wiser if laws about getting married were stricter. When Jesus said 'What God has joined together let no man put asunder', he meant that marriage was so important that it must be taken really seriously. If God himself acts to join two people together, they must be sure that they are making the right choice and that they are both ready to work and suffer to build a really happy marriage with God's help. A broken marriage means great unhappiness and can be disastrous to the children, who grow up without a father or mother, and knowing of the division between their parents.

Can you add to these rules about choosing a wife or husband?

1 Choose someone who is attractive and friendly, but faithful to his or her friends.
2 Look for someone who loves children and intends to share in their upbringing.
3 Find someone who believes in Jesus Christ's teaching about love and marriage.

Most people cannot imagine life without a family. As boys and girls develop and become able to create children of their own, they also have to grow into a sense of responsibility about using this power they have to create new life.

Do you look forward to the time when you will have your own children? How many do you think it is wise to have? What ambitions would you have for them? What kind of home would you like to provide?

Do you know anyone who uses a Family Planning Clinic? Do you know what it is for? Would you go there for advice? Ask your teacher to arrange for a talk or film about Family Planning.

2 Love in society

In order to love someone, you have to be able to understand their problems and find the best way to help them. You have to become involved in their lives. Here are some situations where help is needed because the people concerned cannot help themselves:

1   A sick man has no one to run errands.
2   A pregnant girl is afraid to tell her parents.
3   A woman, living alone with small children, has a badly leaking roof in the wet season.
4   There are mothers with young children who want to go to market on Saturday. They have to leave the children locked up.

Decide the real need in each case and say how you or others could help.

Some people already lead very busy lives, are short of money, and have many responsibilities. Yet they will do as much as they can to help, whereas others will make any excuse to avoid the trouble and effort involved.

Jesus told a parable that sums up the attitude of many people when they are invited to live as members of his Father's community of peace and love and justice:

> One of the men sitting at the table heard this and said to Jesus, 'How happy are those who will sit at the table in the Kingdom of God!'

What's your excuse?

Jesus said to him, 'There was a man who was giving a great feast, to which he invited many people. At the time for the feast he sent his servant to tell his guests, "Come, everything is ready!" But they all began, one after another, to make excuses. The first one told the servant, "I bought a field, and have to go and look at it; please accept my apologies." Another one said, "I bought five pairs of oxen and am on my way to try them out; please accept my apologies." Another one said, "I have just got married, and for this reason I cannot come." The servant went back and told all this to his master. The master of the house was furious and said to his servant, "Hurry out to the streets and alleys of the town, and bring back the poor, the crippled, the blind, and the lame." Soon the servant said, "Your order has been carried out, sir, but there is room for more." So the master said to the servant, "Go out to the country roads and lanes, and make people come in, so that my house will be full. I tell you all that none of those men who were invited will taste my dinner!"' Luke 14, v. 15—24

What kind of excuses would we make today? Often we are not willing to help others, because

—33—

we are not sure of ourselves. When Jesus said, 'Love your neighbour as yourself,' he gave us a very good way of discovering just what standards we are setting ourselves. We can judge by these how they are either helping or hindering our development in relationships with others, particularly those in need.

What do we see when we look at ourselves?

Do we ever really bother to face up to who we are and what we really are aiming to become?

This is a poem by a twelve-year-old girl. Could you write one on the same theme, but using the idea of a mirror as the ideal of what you could be as a person, with hopes and dreams?

When I look at myself in a mirror,
I see myself in many different ways;
Sometimes chubby, sometimes slim,
It's hard to find out what I really look like.
Because a mirror and your eyes
Can play some very nasty tricks on you
Well, look at it this way.
Your eyes might need resting.
And you put it off.
Because you think
Your eyes are just playing
Another trick on you.
When I look in a mirror
I see a reflection of myself
Every time I look in a mirror
I see a very odd and different reflection of myself
I stare and I stare and I stare
Trying to figure out why I look different
Each time I look in a mirror
Until my eyes are fixed
and I am fast asleep.
                    Carol Marsh, St Hilda's High School

At least, the girl who wrote the poem sees herself as one unique person, with many different facets.

She will only learn what kind of person she is as opposed to simply what she looks like in her relationships with her family and friends. Perhaps she will like what she discovers; almost certainly there will be things she will not like.

To learn to love herself — she will not just become selfish! She will become more aware of herself as an individual and value herself as a unique personality with her own contribution to make to the glory of human life.

Some people discover that they are rather afraid of themselves, lack confidence in their abilities, and feel that they are of little real value to anyone. Everyone goes through phases like this but it is certainly not the way to be.

List the ways that you are unique and valuable as a person.

Another reason for people not feeling confident about helping each other and sharing their lives is that there are all kinds of divisions and barriers between people that need to be broken down. Obvious ones are money, education, and jobs, which can cause people to see themselves as a group apart from and above others. Religion can divide a community. Even in the same denomination, groups can have opinions and ideas that conflict with others in the same church. Colour is the most noticeable barrier in the West Indies, though it is less of a barrier now to equality and justice than it is in the Southern United States of America or South Africa. The poet who wrote this poem was deeply aware of the challenge of social change and the need to give society purpose and direction:

> I come from the nigger yard of yesterday
> leaping from the oppressor's hate
> and scorn of myself.
> I come to the world with scars upon my soul,
> Wounds upon my body, fury in my hands
> I turn to the histories of men
> And the lives of people
> I examine the shower of sparks,
> the wealth of dreams.
> I am pleased with the glories,

and sad with the sorrows,
rich with the riches,
Poor with the loss
From the nigger yard of yesterday,
I come with the burden,
to the world of to-morrow,
I turn with my strength.

Martin Carter

Arab-Israeli conflict: Israeli Border Police patrol their frontier with Jordan

Every day there are incidents, on a local or a world-wide scale, that bring home to anyone who is aware of the harm done by divisions, the need for love, the kind of love Christ gave so perfectly.

He taught us to be tolerant of differing personalities and temperaments.

As Jesus and his disciples went on their way, he came to a certain village where a woman named Martha welcomed him in her home. She had a sister named Mary, who sat down at the feet of the Lord and listened to his teaching. Martha was upset over all the work she had to do; so she came and said, 'Lord, don't you care that my sister has left me to do all the work by myself? Tell her to come and help me!'

The Lord answered her, 'Martha, Martha! You are worried and troubled over so many things, but just one is needed. Mary has chosen the right thing, and it will not be taken away from her'.

Luke 10, v. 38–42

Get your priorities right

He showed us the importance of helping at that moment rather than putting it off.

The Lord answered him by saying, 'You hypocrites! Any one of you would untie his ox or his donkey from the stall and take it out to give it water on the Sabbath. Now here is this descendant of Abraham whom Satan has kept in bonds for eighteen years; should she not be freed from her bonds on the Sabbath?' His answer made all his enemies ashamed of themselves, while all the people rejoiced over every wonderful thing that he did.

Luke 13, v. 15–17

Why hesitate?

Jesus! Son of David!

He was immediately open to the cry of anyone in need.

Jesus was coming near Jericho, and a certain blind man was sitting by the road, begging. When he heard the crowd passing by he asked, 'What is this?'

'Jesus of Nazareth is passing by,' they told him.

He cried out, 'Jesus! Son of David! Have mercy on me!'

The people in front scolded him and told him to be quiet. But he shouted even more loudly, 'Son of David! Have mercy on me!'

So Jesus stopped and ordered that the blind man be brought to him. When he came near, Jesus asked him,

'What do you want me to do for you?'

'Sir,' he answered, 'I want to see again'.

Then Jesus said to him, 'See! Your faith has made you well'.

At once he was able to see, and he followed Jesus, giving thanks to God. When the crowd saw it, they all praised God.

Luke 18, v. 35–43

Forgive and forget

He made clear the need for mercy and forgiveness rather than vengeance.

'Teacher,' they said to Jesus, 'this woman was caught in the very act of committing adultery. In our Law Moses gave a commandment that such a woman must be stoned to death. Now, what do you say?' They said this to trap him, so they could accuse him. But Jesus bent over and wrote on the ground with his finger. As they stood there asking him questions, he straightened up and said to them, 'Whichever one of you has committed no sin may throw the first stone at her'. Then he bent over again and wrote on the ground. When they heard this they all left, one by one, the older ones first. Jesus was left alone, with the woman still standing there. He straightened up and said to her, 'Where are they, woman? Is there no one left to condemn you?'

'No one, sir,' she answered.

'Well, then,' Jesus said, 'I do not condemn you either. Go, but do not sin again'.

John 8, v. 4–11

Teenagers are involved in many projects to help those in need, the old, the handicapped, and young children. They also help with projects designed to improve the quality of life in the community. They are important in literacy activities, and in giving new life and ideas to the ideals of the older generation.

Is there a teenage volunteer group of any kind in your district?

If there is a group, is it attached to a Church? If it is, would you join it or not? If not, why not?

Do you think people who do not believe in Jesus Christ as the Son of God can care for others as deeply as Christians do? If they can, why does it matter than you should go to Church?

Do you think it is true that the Holy Spirit of Love is at work in all men and women, boys and girls, even though they may not be aware of this? Can you explain the presence of love, that is totally generous and self-giving in human life, in any other way?

The volunteers themselves learn a great deal from the handicapped people they serve. They see endurance and courage that they might otherwise never have met. The devotion of men and women, whose partners have been made helpless, and of parents for their handicapped children, shows them the best in human love.

Two of the people the boys visit have had both legs amputated. Another lady is not only confined to her wheelchair, but also has her fingers so bent and crippled that they are useless. Yet all three, like so many others, show real strength of character. They have no resentment that life has been so hard. The volunteers find serving them a humbling experience.   L. C. Bailey

Russian children in a Moscow park

It is not enough to care for your family and friends and your immediate neighbours in your community, for we belong to a wider community of different races and nations on a world-wide scale. But is it possible to care for people you have never met nor are likely to meet?

Is it really important to care for the needs of others when our own needs are great?

One reason why it is necessary is that such interest in and awareness of others can help to prevent wars. Sharing resources and talents can build relationships that are not easily broken by the kind of quarrels that caused wars in the past. The aim of the United Nations makes this point very clearly:

> To co-operate internationally in solving international economic, social, cultural, and humanitarian problems, and in promoting respect for human rights and fundamental freedoms.

In the Caribbean area, the work of volunteers from other nations, like America, England and Germany, has been a sign of friendship. West Indians are very important in working for better race relations in England on behalf of the immigrants.

To help to build a more just and loving community, many people join organisations, so that their work can have real and permanent effects. Operation Friendship, Polio Rehabilitation Unit, Jamaica Society for the Prevention of Cruelty to Animals, the Literacy Campaign, Basic Schools, are all in need of help in Jamaica. Similar organisations exist throughout the Caribbean.

Sometimes valuable work can be done on an individual level. The old lady who lives next door will probably prefer help from someone in her own community than from an outsider. There is a good deal of ordinary everyday kindness that never gets organised or recognised.

This is perhaps what Jesus meant particularly when he said:

> So when you give something to a needy person, do not make a big show of it, as the hypocrites do in the synagogues and on the streets. They do it so that

Dunrobin Basic School

people will praise them. Remember this! They have already been paid in full. But when you help a needy person, do it in such a way that even your closest friend will not know about it, but it will be a private matter. And your Father, who sees what you do in private, will reward you.

Matthew 6, v. 2–4

But many people are not involved on either level. This diagram sums up the elements in the situation. How do you score?

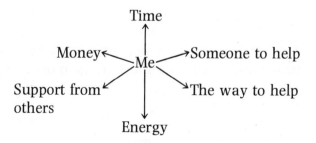

Perhaps it is illuminating to study the way Jesus spent his time, so that we can discover how to be most effective. It is certainly not enough to be kind and well-meaning. This usually leaves people feeling resentful. Often Christ demanded faith and repentance before he agreed to help. He expected people to grow from the point at which he helped them. He only shows the way and gives the strength. But no one who received help from Christ was passive. There had to be active co-operation. This is the only way perhaps that those in need of help can keep their self-respect and dignity.

Christ not only showed us how to work in society to heal all kinds of spiritual and physical hurts with love – he told us that, unless we did live in this way, we should constantly be refusing to love him, and would remain alone in darkness.

> The righteous will then answer him, 'When, Lord, did we ever see you hungry and feed you, or thirsty and give you drink? When did we ever see you a stranger and welcome you in our homes, or naked and clothe you? When did we ever see you sick or in prison, and visit you?' The King will answer back, 'I tell you, indeed, whenever you did this for one of the least important of these brothers of mine, you did it for me!'
>
> Matthew 25, v. 37–40

Can you design a poster asking young people to help with a project for some group in need?

3 Work

A Careers Adviser is in school. You are next to speak to him. What will you say?

Have you any idea which job you would like?

Have you worked or planned for it?

Have you considered some of the following jobs?

Because you are your own master?

Because you can make good money?

Because it gives you status?

Because it means you are creating something beautiful or worthwhile?

Imagine you are a person doing some of the following pieces of work. Say whether you think it is worth doing and what it is contributing to the value of your life and the life of the community. If you feel it has no real value, say so and explain why.

1 Unloading a fishing catch.
2 Cutting bananas.
3 Waiting at table in a tourist hotel.
4 Looking after children while the mother is at work.
5 Teaching an infant class.
6 Sorting vegetables for market.
7 A priest or minister in a small town.
8 Carving wooden figures for sale.
9 Working in a government department.
10 Working for a bank.
11 Working in a library.

Put the following list of jobs in the order of preference which you feel boys and girls would give to them:

A dancer
A professional sportsman
A shop worker
A salesman
A bauxite miner
A public works official

A farmer
A fisherman
A tile-maker
A maid or house boy
A civil servant
A tourist board worker
A church worker

Write about the job which you feel would make you happy. Mention wages, hours, value for others, creative possibilities, future prospects, status.

The following is a prayer that you might say to ask for help and guidance, if you think Jesus would be interested in your plans:

> Lord, there seem to be very few jobs that I feel really interested in doing. I change my mind from day to day. I know that I dream of being rich and famous, about becoming a fantastic pop star or the man who finds enough food for everyone in the world to eat, but I have to prepare myself for reaching the top by doing well the most humble jobs in the beginning. What will be the most satisfying job for me to do?
>
> Help me to decide what will be the most satisfying job for a person like me. I need to use whatever talent I have to the full, without envying those who seem to find it easier to get more money quicker than I do. Give me enough money to live for what I need and a few pleasures, and the unselfishness to use extra money for others as well as myself. Bring me to understand that in whatever job I find myself, consideration for others, justice and friendship will make it worthwhile.   Amen

Jesus had two important jobs in his life. He was a carpenter for much of his life; then he became a rabbi, which is a teacher.

He would have been an important person, first as a skilled workman, and then as a teacher. Today, people find status and a place in their community according to the job they do. Some jobs appear to require a special dedication that seems to come from God, like nursing and teaching. These are called 'vocations', or callings. Some religions use this word when speaking of the job of priest or minister, nuns or church workers.

It's not what you do, but how you do it

It is important to see, however, that every job has its own dignity, and can be given personal value in the way it is performed and in the service it provides for others.

A job worth doing is worth doing well – but how many people today do as little as possible for as much money as possible?

Find examples of work poorly done that causes trouble for and discredit to the person who has performed the task, for example, a badly prepared meal in a restaurant or badly repaired shoes.

In the newspapers, or on the radio or TV, there will probably be news of a strike. Do you think there is a good reason for it?

Quite often trades unions are accused of causing trouble in industry by protecting poor workmen and encouraging claims for more and more money for fewer hours of work. They have also raised standards for workers, and are important in making sure that pay and hours are just.

Ask your teacher if you can invite a trades union official to speak to your class about the way the trades unions work, and how you would join one when you start work.

THE DAILY GLOBE, MONDAY, FEBRUARY 11, 1974

1A. Help Wanted: Male

Urgently Required One Gas Appliance Service-man with at least three (3) years experience. Person should also be able to ride a Scooter bike and work on his own initiative. Apply in person to: K.J. vin for Service Department. Homelect X Limited, 3 Newport Boulevard., Kingston 1.

2. Help Wanted: Female

Wanted an Experienced Barmaid to work in a bar at 8½ Waltham Park Road. Please call Mrs. Smith after 10.00 a.m. any day.

6. Employment Wtd. Household: Female

Two Young Experienced Women Seek positions as general-maids, cooks or laundresses. Ph. 2 27 . No. 1 13

Expatriate Going To Employ Living-in maid. Wants to find job for previous well recommended daily maid. Telephone 6 72 . Sherley.

Middle Aged Woman Seeks Job To work with small family. Call Pearl. 4 Rosalie Ave., Kgn. 1 .

Women Seek Jobs As Cook, Nurse-maid, washer. days-worker, general helper, live in or out. Phone 2 7 1. Mavis.

11A.

Wanted For R school, Claren ral and one T mics for Jan Chairman Sch teacher, Rock River P.O. C

Wanted: Trai ably male) School from teach in Sen available in Rev. B. L. P.O., Manch

Trained Tea All-Age S 1974, traini agriculture copies of

Certain qualities in ourselves can be developed in our work. These are valuable in our growth as people, and they deepen our capacity to live unselfishly and in the service of others:

Honesty	in the use of time and materials, and in the use of the money we earn.
Care	in what we do, so that nothing is wasted, whether it belongs to us or not.
Punctuality	by being there when we are needed.

—53—

Reliability	so that we can be trusted to do things without being watched all the time.
Self-respect	so that we are proud of our achievements, and valued because we contribute by working and giving ourselves as people to the good of our community.

List which of these qualities are important in your life now, and say why.

A very important aspect of work is the people with whom we work. They will be able to make working hours joyful and productive, or miserable and lacking in purpose.

This short extract conveys something of the joy to be gained by working with others:

The young man went to a patch of the burnt canes. The girls came too, standing by to pile the fallen stalks of sweet juice into heaps, so that they could be loaded quickly on to the carts and raced to the weighing bridge. The brothers worked a little apart, silently, swiftly. Burnt cane fell as if a machine were at work. The blades swung in the air, glistened for a moment in the sunlight and descended on the soft stalks near to the roots. Though the work had been started to see who would be the faster, neither of them moved ahead of the other. Sometimes Romesh paused until Hari came abreast, and sometimes Hari waited a few canes for Romesh. Once they looked at each other and laughed together, sweat on their faces getting into their mouths. It was the closest the brothers had ever been since they were children, and to them it was as sweet as the cane they cut.

Samuel Selvon

4 Leisure

Many people see work as an unpleasant necessity. They work only to earn money with which to buy food and clothing, and to make sure that they have money with which to enjoy themselves. This money can be spent on drink, cigarettes, gambling, dancing, or fashionable clothes, all of which are expensive. Can you think of better ways of spending it? What do you like to do in your spare time? Perhaps you like cycling, cricket, fishing, dressmaking, drawing, painting, reading or listening to records?

Most people nowadays have leisure time, unless they are working overtime. Trades unions have achieved quite a lot of control over hours of work. Many people who start work now can expect to be free in the evenings and at weekends, whereas their parents and grandparents could well have worked from dawn until dusk every day.

But how best can we use this freedom?

At school, sport of various kinds, collecting different things, wood carving, drama, and choir activities, are often organised for us.

Our activities will be decided by the time we have available.

Make a timetable of a typical day for a teenage boy or girl. School and jobs at home will probably use up the greater part of the day. Looking after clothes, shoes, hair, etc., should be an important item. It is likely that everyone will have about two or three hours a day that are 'free' to be used as he or she wishes.

Do a survey in your class to find out what everyone does with his leisure time, and perhaps extend it to the school, over a range of ages.

There are some questions you can ask:

How much free time do you have each day or each week?

Do you belong to any clubs?

Do you join in any sport?

Do you spend time each day to pray?

Do you expect to spend any time in Church activities during the week?

Do you think there are enough facilities in your district?

Which do you think is the greatest danger facing teenagers — drink, drugs, smoking, disease?

Do boys and girls spend time together?

The activities that people have in their spare time probably show quite a lot about them. Some people are more organised than others. They like group activities, and may belong to the Boys' Brigade or the Scouts or Guides. Others are quieter and prefer to do things on their own, or perhaps with just one friend. Some may be good at sport, and join cricket or football teams, or take up athletics. School clubs that are organised after school hours can be useful to those who are free to stay. Some people are interested in animals and birds and spend time with pets, or help at an animal clinic. Many girls like looking after small children, or just talking with friends.

Many young people like bright lights, music, and dancing. They like to dress up to go to a dance or to a 'disco'. Listening to records and transistors can be very important to some young people. Pop music and interest in the lives of pop stars is part of present-day teenage culture. Schools and youth clubs run 'discos', where boys and girls can have a good time. Again, the dangers and problems of drink and fights always have to be faced. Why do they happen?

People join youth clubs for different reasons, if they are lucky enough to have one in their area. They want to find company and friends as well as activities.

Write a short description of the kind of club you would like to have in your district.

As girls and boys grow up they want to spend more time together. This is healthy, and contributes a good deal to the fun and interest of leisure time.

To avoid the dangers, a safe rule is to realise that there is safety in numbers. Boy and girl relationships can become too much concentrated on sex, rather than companionship. This can be unfortunate at an age when both boys and girls are developing as persons and need each other. To become mature and to be able to cope with the emotional problems that are part of growing up, involves a need to talk things over and share experiences so that you can grow in the understanding of new responsibilities. It is wise to get to know a lot of different members of the opposite sex rather than 'go steady' too soon.

Enjoying each other's company

Leisure time is meant to be:
    a time of refreshment,
    a time of relaxation,
    a time of renewal.

Bodies and minds have only a certain amount of energy, and without rest and renewal people soon lose their vitality. Without recreation, people become dull and even depressed, so they cannot enjoy themselves when they get the chance.

What do people mean when they say they like a 'good time'? Write about the way you would like to spend your leisure time.

A Prayer

Lord, help me to see the value of
    using my spare time creatively,
Let me find friends who will share
    activities that are worthwhile.
I need to dream, to explore my world, and use all
    my talents.
I need time to talk with friends
    and learn how to act in all kinds of situations,
Give me love and wisdom so that
    I can find real joy in all I do, at all times, anywhere.
Give me strength to fight the temptations that face me
    as I grow up, so that I can always keep
My self-respect.

                                        Amen

5 Christian citizenship

If it turns out
in the end
that we didn't accomplish everything
we set out to —
Well, too bad.
But it won't be
because we spent our lives nit-picking
over pluses and minuses in the Book.
It won't be
because we didn't try
or didn't *care*
or ducked out
on the horror that exists
in so much of *this* world.
Maybe *that's* what
my generation
would accept as 'heaven',
this very world we're living in —
but
transformed
by our
knocking out as much ugliness
as we can
in the time we have.

                                        E. Larsen

A Christian outlook is one that demands a very definite attitude to all our activities. Whatever we do, we are either communicating the love of Christ or not.

Many people, like the Pharisees of the time of Christ, are content with the idea that going to church on Sunday and obeying a few rules will keep them right with God. They do not seem to have realised that every action of theirs during the week also concerns their lives as Christians.

Do you know people who cheat at work, waste time, steal materials, go on strike for unjust causes? It is easy to see among your community those who do not value the money they earn, but spend it on rum or gambling rather than on their families. How many quarrels and fights are there amongst people who would make a point of sitting quietly for a while at church on Sunday?

Jesus was very clear about the connection between our behaviour and our worship of his Father:

So if you are about to offer your gift to God at the altar and there you remember that your brother has something against you, leave your gift there in front of the altar and go at once to make peace with your brother; then come back and offer your gift to God.

Matthew 5, v. 23—24

Perhaps churches would be half empty if we all took this warning completely seriously. In the Sermon on the Mount, Christ used several comparisons to show how important it was for his followers to be a good influence in the world:

You are like salt for all mankind. But if salt loses its taste, there is no way to make it salty again. It has become worthless, so it is thrown away and people walk on it. Matthew 5, v. 13

No one lights a lamp to put it under a bowl; instead he puts it on the lampstand, where it gives light for everyone in the house. In the same way your light must shine before people, so that they will see the good things you do and give praise to your Father in heaven.

Matthew 5, v. 15—16

A city built on a hill cannot be hid.

Matthew 5, v. 14

Jamaican boys and girls are given high ideals in their National Pledge, to inspire them in their Christian lives:

Before God and all mankind, I pledge the love and loyalty of my heart, the wisdom and courage of my mind, the strength and vigour of my body, in the service of my fellow citizens.

I promise to stand up for justice, brotherhood and peace, to work diligently and creatively, to think generously and honestly, so that Jamaica may, under God, increase in beauty, fellowship and prosperity, and play her part in advancing the welfare of the whole human race.

St James gave some practical advice:

My brothers! What good is it for someone to say, 'I have faith,' if his actions do not prove it? Can that faith save him? Suppose there are brothers or sisters who need clothes and don't have enough to eat. What good is there in your saying to them, 'God bless you! Keep warm and eat well!' — if you don't give them the necessities of life? So it is with faith: if it is alone and has no actions with it, then it is dead.

James 2, v. 14—17

In 1968 the Jamaican Government was instrumental in getting the United Nations to organise Human Rights Year, dedicated to making people throughout the world more aware of the dignity and rights of every person of whatever race, colour, or creed.

The United Nations Building, New York

A Christian community is one in which each individual is valued, not only for what he can contribute but for all that he is, as a unique human being. In most countries, basic human rights are safeguarded by the elected government, which appoints ministers to be responsible for development of services, to promote them and maintain respect for them – for example; housing, education, employment, food and agriculture, freedom of religion, freedom of speech, the right to vote.

Do you know the names of ministers in your country who are responsible for these rights? What other government departments are there?

Sometimes a government makes mistakes, or follows policies that favour one group of people rather than another. At election time, all kinds of problems are faced, and promises are made as party leaders try to encourage more people to vote for them.

Unless voters do use their power to vote responsibly, there is bound to be danger that governments become out of touch with their real needs. Christian Church leaders try to encourage everyone to vote, to take proper responsibility for the justice and progress in their own community. It is very easy to grumble and criticise, but not so easy to change things.

At election times, it is obviously important that voters can read and understand what is being said, as well as listen to clever speakers, who can influence them by their talents. It is important that all citizens should follow the activities of the government by reading newspapers. Yet there are many thousands, and indeed millions, of people

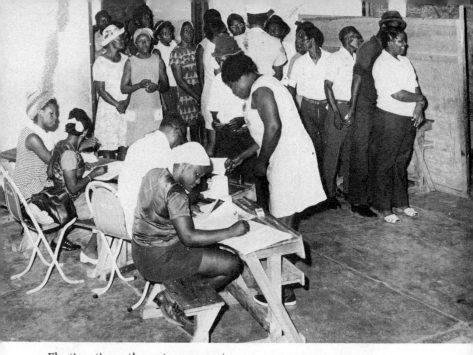

Election time: the votes are cast . . .

. . . the results are announced

in the world who cannot read or write. Sometimes there are opportunities of literacy classes. In some countries these are overcrowded, but in others people may be ashamed to be seen going to the classes. Perhaps we can help everyone to realise the importance of literacy.

What does the word 'Christian' mean to most people? A lot will depend on the Christians that they have met. It would be a pity if the people who run some of the organisations to help the needy and the handicapped were not sure of support from every Christian in the community. Quite often Christians take the lead, but not always. It is often those people who do not seem to have time to go to church who sacrifice hours of their time to run activities to raise money. Can you explain this situation?

The following is a list of some of the charitable organisations in Jamaica. Which of these would you feel should have help from you? Are there other organisations in your area?

Child Welfare Association
St Vincent de Paul Society
Red Cross
Association for the Mentally Handicapped
Cancer Society
Hansen Home for Lepers
Polio Rehabilitation Unit
St John's Ambulance Brigade
Operation Friendship
Basic Schools
Children's Hospital
Legion
Salvation Army School for the Blind
4 H Clubs

Every year there is a big campaign in Jamaica
to raise money for all these charities, known as
'Nuggets for the Needy'. In 1969 there was a
target of $70,000. At the end of the campaign,
there is a big entertainment, which is seen by
thousands on television. The whole country is
united in interest in the events, and many people
are very generous.

A $2,500 cheque, raised by the Nuggets for the Needy
Campaign, is received for the extension of the Blood Bank

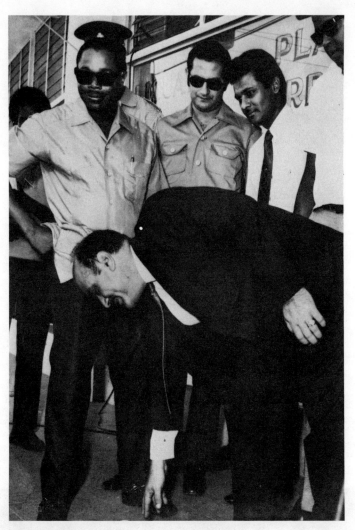

The first link in a Nuggets Chain is made

Can you ask your teacher if you can have a speaker from one of these organisations to help you learn more about it? Collect pictures and articles from newspapers to make a collage. If different members of the class write to the organisations, a class scrapbook of information can be made. Perhaps you can organise a school service about the responsibilities everyone has as a Christian citizen.

There are many occasions when Jesus made clear to us that it does matter if we ignore our duties to others, especially if, at the same time, we insist on our own rights and freedom.

Here are two examples of the kind of people who need to hear what he had to say — but do you think they will listen?

A family have a nice home and all the children are well looked after and do well at school. But they are like the children in this poem:

My Parents Kept Me from Children who were Rough

My parents kept me from children who were rough
And who threw words like stones and who wore
   torn clothes
Their thighs showed through rags. They ran in the
   streets
And climbed cliffs and stripped by the country
   streams.

I feared more than tigers their muscles like iron
Their jerking hands and their knees tight on my arms.
I feared the salt coarse pointing of those boys
Who copied my lisp behind me in the road.

They were lithe, they sprang out behind hedges
Like dogs to bark at my world. They threw mud
And I looked another way, pretending to smile
I longed to forgive them, but they never smiled.

Stephen Spender

Do you think they would have helped the Samaritan on the road to Jericho? Read the story again:

Jesus answered: 'There was a man who was going down from Jerusalem to Jericho, when robbers attacked him, stripped him and beat him up, leaving him half dead. It so happened that a priest was going down that road; when he saw the man he walked on by, on the other side. In the same way a Levite also came there, went over and looked at the man, and then walked on by, on the other side. But a certain Samaritan who was travelling that way came upon him, and when he saw the man his heart was filled with pity. He went over to him, poured oil and wine on his wounds and bandaged them; then he put the man on his own animal and took him to an inn, where he took care of him. The next day he took out two silver coins and gave them to the innkeeper. "Take care of him," he told the innkeeper, "and when I come back this way I will pay you back whatever you spend on him." ' And Jesus concluded, 'In your opinion, which one of these three acted like a fellow-man towards the man attacked by the robbers?' The teacher of the Law answered, 'The one who was kind to him'. Jesus replied, 'You go, then, and do the same'.

Luke 10, v. 30–37

A boy belongs to a family, in which the father is out of work and the mother does not spend enough time looking after the home. Many people feel it is a lazy, good-for-nothing family. Do you think the boy will grow up to be a thief and a bad citizen? Would he bother to vote if, all his life, no one in the community has shown any real interest in him?

Read St Matthew's Gospel, Chapter 25, verses 31–46.

The Last Judgement

6 Decisions

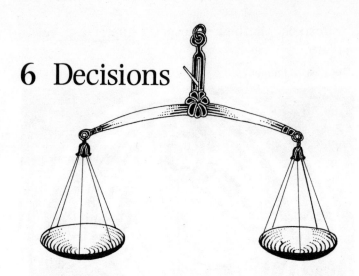

It is often difficult, as we live through each day, to feel that we are very involved in the larger problems of society. Life is often a struggle to survive, to keep fit and healthy, to do a job properly, and to maintain a reasonably friendly relationship with people around us.

Yet we are very much affected by the values of the society in which we live. We can be influenced a great deal in our attitudes to our goals in life. We constantly have to make decisions because of the challenges and conflicts that are offered by people with different standards. How do you make up your mind?

Do you do what you have always done?
Do you do what your parents would do?
Do you ask advice from your friends?
Do you write to a newspaper or magazine?

Is there a teacher or youth leader or a minister or priest who can help you?

This is an important series of questions, because adolescence is a difficult period. Although you no longer look like a child, you probably behave like one sometimes and other people may perhaps treat you as one. On the other hand, you will be expected to be more responsible and grown-up, and yet find yourself in trouble if you try to build up a life of more independence and freedom that seems to break the rules of the adult world.

A great deal of adjustment to a more adult approach to life will depend on early training and upbringing.

Young children are very dependent on adults. They do not have the knowledge or experience necessary for making decisions. But this does not mean that, as they grow, they should not be trained to make decisions for themselves. This means that they have to be trusted and guided, and not simply punished if they do wrong so that they obey out of fear, instead of understanding the meaning and effects of what they do. There are four methods of training: (i) physical punishment; (ii) rewards for good behaviour; (iii) loss of privileges; (iv) reasoning.

The first three methods are useful for immediate correction of behaviour, yet they do not always develop a good relationship. If it is possible for the person in authority and the young person to discuss the conflict and see the reasons for it and the best way to solve it, then there will be better conditions in which maturity can develop.

1   Some people can point the way.

2   Some people light the way.

3   Others explain the best way to get there.

4   **You make the decision!**

1

2

Although young people often resent the influence of home, school, community, and country in their lives and feel that they have no real freedom to make their own decisions, it is only if they break away entirely from this structure and try to live a 'drop out' or 'hippy' kind of life that they may realise how lonely they are.

We need the support of others, especially in making difficult decisions, and we need love and approval and appreciation from the groups to which we belong. Even then, we are alone at times, facing problems and difficulties that seem impossible. It is at this point that we can share Christ's feelings in Gethsemane. He knew he was likely to be arrested and put to death, and he had to choose whether to stay and face this or to run away. He asked his friends to pray with him, but they fell asleep.

Do you ever feel that no-one is really interested in your problems? Are people too busy to listen?

At least Christians can pray as Christ did and get some comfort from knowing that, if they do what they know is right, God our Father will be with them. Even though we may get plenty of help, ultimately we have to be alone before God in making a decision.

3

4

Jesus faces his decision, alone in Gethsemane

Lord, help me to face the times when I have to make decisions that will mean hardship. Give me strength to rely on myself and to realise that no one else can take responsibility for my actions. If I have to accept tragic or challenging events in my life, may I remember that you were able to find enough courage to do so.

When I feel most alone, may I realise that you understand and are close to me.   Amen

What do you really want?

This isn't easy to discover, but it is vital that aims and goals should be thought out, or else life simply becomes aimless or an escape.

Of course it can be easier to drift, and human beings have various ways of avoiding real decisions and responsibilities.

There is the 'Play-it-safe' type:

'I go to Church on Sunday.'
'My children aren't going to play with those rough children.'
'My home is always clean and tidy.'
'I don't smoke.'
'I pay cash for all I buy.'

There is the 'Playboy' type:

'Life is beautiful – I can't stand anything ugly or unhappy.'
'Handicapped people make me feel ill.'
'I didn't enjoy that party – not enough drink.'
'Wonder if I'll meet a new girl/boy to-night? Last night I wasn't so lucky.'
'Why do girls/boys get serious?'
'If that horse wins, I'll be in the money!'

There is the 'Run-away' type:

'Does he think I'll do that homework? It would take all night!'
'Drugs are good fun.'
'Who cares about working? You can always get government assistance!'
'I've fathered three children and don't pay a penny towards their keep!'

Most of us have some of these tendencies – the demands of life are great, and it is not always easy to face up to the constant self-sacrifice that is expected of us. It does help, if we train ourselves in small ways. If you have a homework assignment, is it easier to watch television? What happens in school the next day?

You go to a party and get drunk or smoke ganga. How do you feel when you find your mother is waiting for you when you return home?

Perhaps the answer to both these questions would be a 'don't care' one. Without some kind of pressure or influence this can remain the attitude towards many important issues, when faced with choosing between right and wrong because someone else has told you what to do, and you do not feel really involved.

Somewhere there is a dream of truth, goodness, and happiness that is reached only after constant struggle and out of love. People know that 'being good' is a sham if it is only a law-keeping exercise. It is really an achievement if consideration for others, and truly creative activity, results in a growth in love and maturity that is a light in the darkness for those who see little purpose in life. Sometimes it is 'evil' that seems a threat and a challenge that dares you to act. 'Good' seems only to mean conformity, giving in, dullness, and boredom.

Christ's challenge was one of love – and he warned us that this would involve dangers and risks that make sin seem rather tame – but his way of life is the rewarding one.

If there is something you can really do, what a lot of other things you can learn to do, too! If you don't try to do something, you won't be able to do anything!

If you want to help me you must give all your heart to it. You must put yourself last. You must be ready to let people do their worst to you. And you must keep your eyes on me.

Nobody can work for two masters. He will think less of one than he does of the other; or he will be devoted to one, and have no use for the other. Either God is your master — or money is.

Living in God's Way sometimes takes all the courage you've got. You'll be all right — if you never give in.

If you are always thinking of saving your skins, that's just what you won't do. But, if you forget all about yourself because you are keen on helping me, even if you lose your life, you will be all right. You will really be yourself.

Trans. Alan T. Dale

What would be the biggest challenge you have to face if you choose any of the following ways of life?

Some people will be content to follow the path laid down by their parents in their local community.

Others may feel the challenge of 'big-city' living, with wider interests and opportunities.

It may be necessary for others to decide to emigrate if they feel that there is not enough scope for their talents in their own country.

Are you needed in the Caribbean?

So many educated and skilled people leave their local communities, where they are needed in health and education services particularly. There

is a great demand for help in curing ignorance and apathy, in putting an end to resentment against injustice by building happier communities.

In any area in the world, the ideals and energy of young people are vital to the future.

Do you think too many of them soon decide it is easier to be selfish?

To make a decision you have to think clearly, understand what you are doing, and be free to choose.

Here is a list of points to think about:

1 'When the going gets tough, the tough gets going!' Would this saying have made Peter feel upset after he denied Christ? Read John 21, v. 15–19.
2 What is the difference between short-range and long-range goals?
3 In Jamaica and other countries, sports writers claim that young people have the ability to be world class, but don't have enough determination to train. Do you agree?
4 Which project or achievement has given you most satisfaction? How did the fact that it was difficult help to make it more satisfying for you?

(*opposite*) Two nurses from the University Hospital, Kingston

7 Pressures and values

Would you believe it?
Could you believe it?
Should you believe it?

Facts and opinions pour out from mass media —
from newspapers, radio, television. They form
ideas and attitudes and influence behaviour.
Do people question the truth of what they hear
or see? Or think about the people who are pro-

ducing the material and wonder why they go to so much trouble?

Newspapers have had a tremendous influence on society as more and more people have learned to read and take an interest in local and international affairs. But many people buy them for other reasons also — they expect them to be entertaining and interesting and often turn to the comic strips or women's page first. Sensational headlines and 'juicy' crime news also have a big appeal and influence sales.

Can you rely on the facts they give?

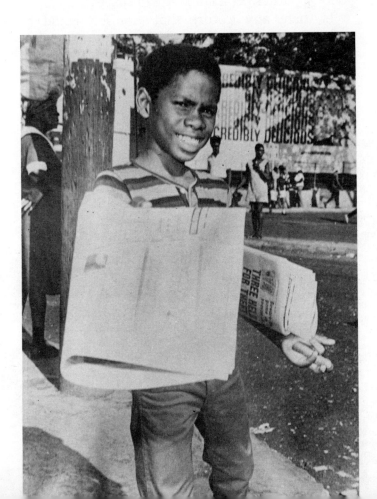

Some newspapers have a world-wide reputation for being impartial and fair like *The Times* in England, and *New York Times* in America. Compare the newspapers in your country. Make an analysis of the space they give to different kinds of news — home news, overseas news, crime, general interest, advertising, comic strips, women's news, children's news, pictures, readers' letters.

Write about what you feel is valuable about newspapers. How can they be dangerous?

Why is it important that there should be an independent Press Council to deal with criticisms and complaints? Who controls newspapers? Do all political parties get a fair share of space?

Is there any feature that you feel could be improved?

It is hard to imagine the world before radio. All communication, except telegraphs, was by print or by word of mouth. Today, people can express their views and provide entertainment for each other over vast distances. Because of television, the spoken word is given much more power with pictures of events as they happen. No one has calculated how many hours are spent in watching TV, but if you have a set or know another family with a set, or watch TV in school, you will know how fascinating it can be.

Both these means of communication have great power for good and evil, and the world community has entered a new era. We know so much more of the way of life in other countries, and can share ideas and discoveries to improve the quality of life in many new ways. Using this survey, analyse your own attitude and try to find out if people you know are benefiting from radio and TV, and discover the problems they can raise.

1 Which programmes do you listen to or watch every week?
2 Which programmes do you enjoy the most?
3 Which programme do you feel is the most educational?
4 Do you think the news is well presented, locally and internationally?
5 Which programme do you feel could be a dangerous influence?
6 Do you ever watch religious programmes on TV? Do you think they could be improved?
7 Do you ever read reviews of programmes or try to criticise them?

A favourite way of spending an evening in some places is a visit to the movies. Films are made for entertainment. Some of them cost millions of dollars. Great stars have become internationally famous and make a great deal of money. They can give us a share in the lives of all kinds of people.

Which is the most popular film that you know?
Who is the greatest film star that you have heard about or seen?
Is there any film you would like to see?

However, films are also blamed for encouraging violence, and too much interest in the wrong kind of sex. They certainly can give a glamorous view of wrong-doing.

Many people think that really dangerous films should be banned. Others feel that people should be given the chance to make up their own minds.

This is a list of scenes that have been shown on the screen:

1 A gunman shoots up three policemen and gets away unhurt.
2 A man and woman have intercourse when they have no real personal relationship.
3 A girl is raped.
4 A hold-up gang beats up two people and takes a lot of money.
5 A terrorist makes petrol bombs so that it is easy to follow his example if you watch carefully.

Can you write down a list of reasons why these films should or should not be shown? Does your list agree with those of your friends?

Advertising is a powerful way of building up a self-image. Using clever methods, advertising firms can encourage you to see yourself in an exciting and glamorous situation. Although, for them, it may only be a means of making money by making sure that you will buy their product, for you, it can be a source of real conflict and temptation.

In learning to sell to our subconscious, another area the merchandisers began to explore carefully, was that involving our secret miseries and self-doubts. They concluded that the sale of billions of dollars worth of products hinged to a large extent upon successfully manipulating or coping with our guilt feelings, fears, anxieties, hostilities, loneliness, feelings, inner tensions.

Vance Packard

Everyone wants the best of everything for themselves and their families, and one big danger from advertising is that it will make it all seem too easy to get and so vital to happiness.

Some products may be better than others, but it is important that people know the tricks that are used to capture interest and promote sales.

For example,

There are a number of techniques which ad-men use to increase the attractiveness of their products; the careful choice of brand name, and the words used to describe the product; the way of life with which it is associated in the advert; the suggestion that a family's not a really happy one without it; the before-and-after method; the recommendation by a famous personality; repetition; the suggestion that the product has aristocratic or scientific connections; jingles.

E. Rudinger and V. Kelly

Check the adverts you see and decide how they are making their appeal. Which has the most effect on you?

Most people have a very healthy attitude to the activities of the mass media and just laugh at them. Perhaps they are able to look at things through Christ's eyes?

Check on these quotations and use them as a focus for discussing or writing about the purpose and dangers of advertising so that fair judgements can be made:

Matthew 6, v. 19–33   Does it profit a man to gain clothes, TV sets, cars, etc., if that is all he has in life?

Luke 22, v. 24—27	It is not the status-seeker but the servant who will be truly honoured.
II Corinthians 12, v. 7—10	Material goods can't always help in pain or trouble.
Phillipians 3, v. 8—14	What really does matter?
Colossians 1, v. 9—12	What really brings happiness — grabbing for yourself or serving your neighbour?

Magazines and comics are also inviting you into their world. Is it very different from your own? Would you really like to live in it? Perhaps some people really believe it is a real world and are constantly disappointed or surprised if they do not meet glamorous men and women, find fabulous homes, or if they discover that 'tough guy' behaviour seems to have different results in real life.

1 Do people ever try to prove they are 'super heroes' in your school or town? How do they do it?

2 Does violence help people to make their own rules? Or do they finally discover that the rules most people agree with are stronger than they are?

3 Do victims of violence deserve it? Why do people who are trying to prove their strength find it tempting to attack the old and the weak?

4 Have you ever had to face real violence? What is the best way to deal with it? Would you use violence yourself? Is it ever right to use it?

Without scientific developments and discoveries, our world would be a very different place. Some have been of great value — medical science has given new hope in sickness, for example.

Because of the work of scientists, people have much more confidence in their ability to interpret and understand the universe, and make better use of its resources. New methods of growing food, of providing fuel and building materials, are making better living conditions slowly available in many parts of the world.

Some people, though, may become over-confident and feel that everything can be explained, and all human problems can be solved, by all the knowledge and skill that science can provide in improving life on this planet.

There are levels of human experience that are difficult to explore through scientific observation and calculation. How can you measure beauty, love, or truth? A new make-up can be produced,

The beauty of this flower . . .

. . . cannot be measured in a laboratory

but its effects are neither deep nor lasting. We do not call in a scientist to prove that two people are in love. Our emotions and intentions are far too complex and difficult to judge – our only insight comes as the result of actions. We cannot prove the truth of what we believe by reason alone. Our view of truth will be different in some way from that of others. In the same way, we cannot prove the existence of God by reason alone – we must judge by what we believe he does.

Great harm has been done to the religious faith of many people by a misunderstanding of how science can help us in understanding the mystery of human existence.

On the spiritual level, some people do find it possible to pray with real sincerity of belief in a response from God. Their understanding of what they can know of life and the universe has led them to realise that there are mysteries that the spirit of man must constantly explore. The existence of the loving spirit of God is something they constantly find proved in all kinds of circumstances.

Perhaps it is the destructive effect of too great a faith in science as the answer to human problems that has led to the growth of the new philosophy of 'existentialism' in this century. This claims that there is nothing beyond this life and that loneliness and suffering are the permanent state of man. This is a terrifying idea, and leads to an attack on morality and religion, for surely we have the right to do anything we like to survive and obtain some happiness in such a world – or so the existentialist might claim.

One reason for the loss of faith is the claim that no one can 'prove' the existence of God. In fact, of course, no one has ever been able to do so, for God lives an existence that is beyond the reach of our ordinary senses.

Our only real contact with Him has been through Jesus Christ who, as an historical figure, has made possible a link with an eternal being on a human level, by living a human life himself.

There are so many problems and conflicts in learning to live with and accept the reality of Jesus that some people just give up, hoping that they may understand some day. Others have rejected the whole idea of any other kind of existence as a fairy story. But in rejecting Christ on this level, people can also reject what he stands for – peace, love, joy, and hope. For them, human life is simply a not too successful struggle for survival with no real potential for change and transformation. It is so obvious that people on their own do not have the resources that can lead to greater justice and happiness.

Can you think of examples of action by people

like Martin Luther King, which might help them to find a little hope? Read the following prayer. Do you agree with what it says?

Reflection

A few men said
that God was dead
and some men started weeping.
A number hoped
that God was doped
and started celebrating.
But many fear
the day is near
when God will be forgotten.
And so it's time again, God,
great and good and one God,
to show yourself again.
Expose yourself in Jesus Christ,
and show yourself
in the heaven above,
in the earth below,
and deep in us.
Show yourself
in the Word of God,
in your sons we meet,
and deep in us.
Show yourself
as you have done before.
Show us enough
to strengthen our faith,
our jittery hearts,
our searching minds,
our buckling knees,
and make your promise sure.
Be God, God
Be God.

Interrobang

There is one science that is directly concerned with human destiny on a rather supernatural level. This is astrology – the study of the movement of stars and planets and their influence on human life.

It is possible that many people you know like to read their horoscopes. Perhaps you do this yourself and often find that things work out. But is this just luck? Can the people who write them really know what is going to happen to each individual born at a certain time in the whole world? It is important to get this into perspective, as much unhappiness can be caused by too great a reliance on predictions.

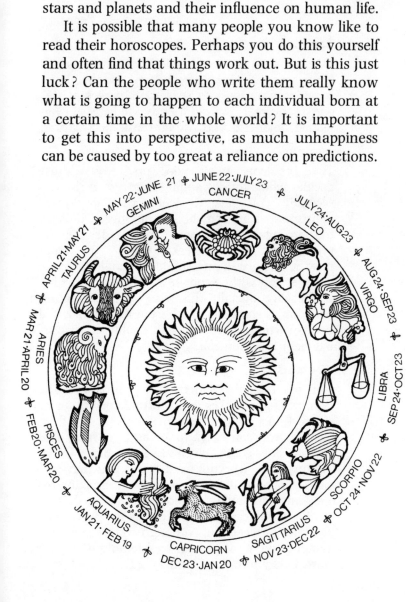

Compare these three predictions. They are taken from three different sources on the same day for those born under the sign of Aquarius:

1 Aquarius

This is a restless time for you because Aquarians always want to make a fresh start, and the planet is undergoing its own seasonal changes at this part of the year. But old friends will be best, even an old boyfriend you thought was past caring.

2 Aquarius

Two problems await you: firstly, you must decide what to do about changes at home; secondly, you have to deal with a display of temperament in somebody you love. Don't be too strong-minded about this – try to be sympathetic. An easy week at work – you should now be doing well and conditions could be made even easier with someone's help on Thursday and Friday. Socially this week might be rather flat; don't expect too much from it. Letters add a heart-warming note and you could get encouragement from somebody.

3 Aquarius

You are ruled by Saturn and Uranus, and the dual rulership makes you contradictory in many ways. Under Saturn, which is now acting from Gemini, you can be cautious and you may find things slow-going, even a little dull. Under Uranus, now working from Libra, you may surprise people by defying convention, breaking old ties and displaying eccentricity or flashes of genius. If you can, it is best to stick to a systematic working programme. Although romance is very much to the fore, it needs cool handling on your part. Lucky birthday: January 21.

Answer these questions:

1 Which one would you have liked to believe if you were the person concerned?
2 Can you explain the difference, if the stars are supposed to tell the truth about the future?
3 Are people likely to believe what is said because they want to believe it, rather than concern themselves with the problem of whether the material is true or not?
4 Some possible reasons for believing in horoscopes are that (a) people are hungry for security, (b) they are anxious about what is going to happen to them, or, (c) they prefer to be told what to do or expect by others, rather than take the trouble to work things out for themselves. Which reason do you think is the most likely?

This belief in the power of the stars to establish personality or dictate events is very old and primitive, and is really a kind of superstition. A superstition means trusting in objects or persons to influence events, rather than having faith in the loving power of God and your own power of choice.

There are warnings of the dangers of superstition in the Bible:

When you raise your eyes to heaven, when you see the sun, the moon, the stars, all the array of heaven, do not be tempted to worship them and serve them. Yahweh your God has allotted them to all the peoples under heaven, but as for you, Yahweh has taken you, and brought you out from a furnace of iron, from Egypt, to be a people all his own, as you still are to-day.

Deuteronomy 4, v. 19–20

Then we shall not be children any longer, or tossed one way and another and carried along by every wind of doctrine, at the mercy of all the tricks men play and their cleverness in practising deceit. If we live by the truth and in love, we shall grow in all ways into Christ, who is the head by whom the whole body is fitted and joined together, every joint adding its own strength, for each separate part to work according to its function. So the body grows until it has built itself up, in love.

Ephesians 4, v. 14–16

Can you make a list of the other ways in which people try to make sure that life will be good to them? (e.g. touch wood).

A Prayer for trust in God

God my Father, although I am used to hearing people say that you create all things and guide all people in a loving plan for happiness, I still feel insecure. No other human being can know why and how things happen for me, so I do not really believe the horoscopes I read. Help me to study the pattern of events in my life for myself, to see in them a constant call to live in peace and joy, knowing of your love for me, through your son, Jesus Christ.

Amen

In some ways, belief in the stars is a kind of escapism from a world where nothing seems certain. It is not so easy to escape from the influence of your own friends and contemporaries, as you might hope. Human beings are social creatures, they grow and develop through contact with their own kind and are greatly affected by the relationship they have with others.

Usually each new generation has its own challengs to the standards and way of life of the adult world. This is healthy and can do good, but can also be destructive.

The gang gets together

Can you discover whether the attitudes that shock the older generation now are very different from those of your parents at your age? Ask them what kind of conflicts they had with their own parents over hairstyles, clothes, slang, music, smoking, staying out late, sexual freedom, the colour question, drinking, and swearing.

You will probably find that things have basically changed very little. Your parents had to come to terms, as you do, with the things that really matter.

Some aspects of teenage life are always dangerous because freedom is a big responsibility. Many boys and girls feel they have to learn by experience, but some mistakes can be very expensive.

> The teenager still needs his peer group. He needs the company of and membership of his own age group, but this is now sought not for itself; he needs his peers more for the support and protection they can offer, as his still insecure personality hesitantly struggles to emerge. This is the gang stage, proper.
>
> Dorothy Berridge

Is this true in your own experience? How do you choose your gang?

Can you imagine yourself standing out against general teenage standards?

If 'everybody does it', can it be wrong?

Should people try to be different?

How can we judge people and by what standards?

Jesus Christ gave some sound advice:

Sawdust and log

Why do you see a little speck of sawdust in your friend's eye, but not notice the great log of wood in your own eye?

'Tom!' you say to your friend, 'let me take that little speck of dust out of your eye'.

But you yourself don't see the great log of wood in your own eye.

When you act like this, you are only pretending to be good. Take the great log of wood out of your own eye first. Then you will be able to see clearly enough to take the little speck of sawdust out of your friend's eye.

Trans. Alan T. Dale

How big is the log in your eye?

8 Barriers

Race and colour

These are prayers that might be used by people in England, where some people are worried about the divisions caused there by race and colour. There are two sides to the problem.

English people might say:

Lord, help me to understand and appreciate my neighbours whose colour and way of life is different from mine. I know that they are men and women like us, your children too, but they so often act differently from us that I find this hard to believe. Their cooking smells different, they chatter loudly, they are so noisy that it is hard for me not to complain about them. Help me to understand their way of life, and see the good things in it and by being tolerant come to love them for your sake.

Amen

An immigrant might say:

God, it's awful to be black in this country full of white people. It's not that everyone is unfriendly, though some are. It's just so different from home — ideas, ways, talk, laughter. I'm an alien, an exile, however much I try. And then sometimes Lord, they seem to hate me, and then I hate them back for all their superiority and whiteness. Lord, help me to understand and be understood.

Amen

Is it fair that anyone should be judged by the colour of their skin?

Can you explain why any one group, black or white, should think that they are superior to another?

In some parts of the world, racial division is more terrible in its effects than it is in the Caribbean.

Cape Town, Sunday

A Durban family will have to split up because the husband has failed to obtain official classification as a white man according to Mr Michael Mitchell, an Opposition United Member of Parliament.

The father had now been classified as a Coloured (mixed race). His wife was classified as white. Their seven children will also be officially regarded as Coloured, as a recently passed race law lays down that children with one non-white parent would not be classified as white.

Mr Mitchell said that the father and the children would probably have to live apart from the mother because Whites and Coloureds are not permitted to live in the same residential area. 'This is the rotten stage we have reached in this country,' he said. 'I cannot see how a measure such as this can be justified on Christian, moral, or even racial grounds. It is inhuman and sickening.'

Do you think this kind of situation could happen in the Caribbean?

Bitterness and hate is real and some feel it deeply, like the man who wrote this poem:

Poor people!
Starving people!
Naked people!
Black
downtrodden
suffering people!

The arc of justice
is at the root of the tree
Come forth!
Come forth, my people!

Let every voice
shout
so loud that it
cannot be ignored.
Strike back,
Strike back, my people!
Let every blow insult our freedom!

Those who withhold relief,
Shall sense the bitterness of grief
The wicked, who exploit the poor,
Shall, even as dust on the floor,
be swept in panic on the mind;
then they shall know how they have sinned.

Let us demand our rights of birth
And assert our claim to this bit of earth
Here,
we renounce the role
of the wretched
of this earth.

Some people are afraid that racial conflict will
become the greatest problem in the world, causing
war and oppression.

Do you think it is an impossible ideal to follow
the Christian teaching in St Paul's letter to the
Galatians?

You were baptised into union with Christ, and so have taken upon yourselves the qualities of Christ himself. So there is no difference between Jews and Gentiles, between slaves and free men, between men and women; you are all one in union with Christ Jesus.

Galatians 3, v. 27—28

Can you suggest other answers to racial tension than violence? What is the answer to poor living conditions, few jobs, contempt as a person?

Could it be prayer . . .
and love?

The benches were packed with Puerto Ricans, negroes, and Italians; among them men and women who would normally never enter a church: the drunk, the thief, the outcast of society. Just the kind of company Jesus kept. It is time for the prayer of intercession, and the minister asks, 'What prayers shall we offer to God today?' There is a pause. Then a Puerto Rican stands up: 'The landlord promised the Christian Action Group he'd fix the plumbing in Betsie's apartment. Signed the agreement too. We ought to thank God.' Another pause. Then twenty-year-old Josh is on his feet: 'Maybe we could pray for the families who'll be baptised next week?' Old Luigi rises, leaning heavily on his stick: 'Supposing there was another gang-fight like last night, I mean, just supposing'. The uneasy stir is broken by another voice. And another. Then: 'Let us pray'.

The pastor turns to the white communion table, looks up at the wooden cross that hangs on the deep-red wall, and then he kneels to offer the prayers of the courageous, the strong, the rejected, the weak, the despised: those who, together, are discovering how social and spiritual chaos can be fought and overcome.   Bruce Kenrick

Rich and poor

A man
was starving
in Capri;
He moved
his eyes
and looked
at me;
I felt
his gaze,
I heard
his moan,
And knew
his hunger
as my own.

Edna St Vincent Millay

This is a list of reasons for poverty. Some of them are probably true of the area in which you live. Put them in the order in which they apply.

Can you see how the situation can be altered?

1 Lack of employment.
2 Laziness.
3 Bad use of money when it has been earned.
4 Misfortune caused by illness or natural disaster, like flood or hurricane.
5 A few people control jobs and money and make a fortune, while others have to manage on a very small wage.
6 Inefficient government that does little to provide better work prospects and housing conditions.

Israelite leaders were deeply concerned with the problem in the life of their nation.

> You must not pervert justice in dealing with a stranger or an orphan, nor take a widow's garment in pledge.
> Remember you were a slave in Egypt and that Yahweh your God redeemed you from there. That is why I lay this charge on you.
> When reaping the harvest in your field, if you have overlooked a sheaf in your field, do not go back for it. Leave it for the stranger, the orphan and the widow.
>
> Deuteronomy 24, v. 17–19

Listen to this, you who trample on the needy and try to suppress the poor people of the country, you who say 'When will the New Moon be over so that we can sell our corn, and sabbath, so that we can market our wheat?'

Then by lowering the bushel, raising the shekel, by swindling and tampering with the scales, we can buy up the poor for money, and the needy for a pair of sandals, and get a price even for the sweepings of the wheat.' Yahweh swears it by the pride of Jacob, 'Never will I forget a single thing you have done'.

Amos 8, v. 4–7

Yet people still give respect to those who are wealthy and they gain high positions in society, even though they may have earned some of their money dishonestly.

If poor people become rich, they are often as selfish and greedy as some of the people they criticise.

Make a list to show the differences in life for the rich and the poor. Which of them causes the most bitterness?

Rich	**Poor**
1 Food to waste	Hunger
2 Fresh, new clothes	Shabby dress

Finish the list.

One big difference is usually the level of education. In the past, education of a good standard has only been available through payment of fees. This situation is changing slowly, and better free education is becoming available for all who want it. But the barriers it can raise will still exist. Have you noticed any of the following problems in your own community?

Aims	Good effects	Bad effects
Knowledge	No more harmful ignorance	Know-all attitude
Social polish	Considerate, civilised behaviour	Snobbery
Good job	Using talents fully	Look down on the less fortunate
New ideas	Open-minded, tolerant and ready to change for the better	Go to extremes, reject everything, whether good or bad
Independence	Able to stand on own feet and make mature decisions	Ready to break away from parents and background altogether

The following is a description of two students with problems. Could you advise them?

Case No 1

A student never takes his friends home, because his parents cannot read or write and his home is poor.

Case No 2

A student finds she cannot talk to her parents any more, as they do not take an interest in anything wider than the details of everyday life and do not understand her problems.

Culture

The word 'culture' has various meanings. It can be used to describe people of high intellectual and artistic refinement. It also means the social, artistic, and intellectual development of a group, the level of civilisation and material achievement that has been reached.

In one country, there may be several clearly defined groups with their own way of life. Often there is a division between those who live in town and country. Can you think of differences in dress, work, leisure, and religious activity in some of the groups in your country?

In the last few years it has sccmcd likcly that customs from the past may disappear very quickly, for society itself, all over the world, is changing quickly. A world-wide civilisation, based on the achievements of the great industrial areas of America and Europe, has spread to all parts of the globe. This has affected young people particularly. Wherever they go, teenagers can be sure of finding others dréssed in the same kind of clothes, listening to the same kind of music, trying drink and drugs, experimenting with life on all

levels, discussing the same kind of problems, drinking Coke and Pepsi.

In many ways they are living in their own world, and are more in touch with the vast changes that are taking place than their parents are. They are inheriting also doubts and fears that have grown up about beliefs and standards based on Christianity. These have been challenged by science, by social injustice, by the threat of nuclear war. Can there possibly be a loving God? Do standards matter, when they can seem to divide and torture people who need, above all, to love and be loved?

Perhaps there is great hope for the world in the unity that is growing amongst people of different nations. Perhaps the religion that is being rejected was not a true religion?

Religion should not be narrow and exclusive. Christ said:

> How terrible for you, teachers of the Law and Pharisees! Hypocrites! You lock the door to the Kingdom of heaven in men's faces, but you yourselves will not go in, and neither will you let people in who are trying to go in!
>
> Matthew 23, v. 13

Religion should not be centred on the next world. Jesus said:

> Some Pharisees asked Jesus when the Kingdom of God would come. His answer was, 'The Kingdom of God does not come in such a way as to be seen. No one will say, "Look, here it is!" or, "There it is!"; because the Kingdom of God is within you.'
>
> Luke 17, v.21

Religion should not be too concerned with God and not other people. One of Jesus' friends said:

> Dear friends! Let us love one another, because love comes from God. Whoever loves is a child of God and knows God. Whoever does not love does not know God, because God is love.
>
> I John 4, v. 7–8

Do you remember this song by the New Seekers? A good prayer, perhaps?

> I'd like to teach the world to sing in perfect harmony
> I'd like to hold it in my arms and keep it company
> I'd like to build the world a home
> And furnish it with love
> With apple trees and honey bees
> And snow white turtle doves.

9 Authority

Outside, even through the shut window-pane, the world looked cold. Down in the street little eddies of wind were whirling dust and torn paper into spirals, and though the sun was shining and the sky a harsh blue, there seemed to be no colour in anything, except the posters that were plastered everywhere. The black-moustachio'd face gazed down from every commanding corner. There was one on the house-front immediately opposite. BIG BROTHER IS WATCHING YOU, the caption said, while the dark eyes looked deep into Winston's own. Down at street level another poster, torn at one corner, flapped fitfully in the wind, alternately covering and uncovering the single word INGSOC. In the far distance a helicopter skimmed down between the roofs, hovered for an instant like a bluebottle, and darted away again with a curving flight. It was the police patrol, snooping into people's windows. The patrols did not matter, however. Only the Thought Police mattered.

The above extract is from George Orwell's novel, 1984, written in 1949, which made very clear the dangers of dictatorship. Authority can do great harm to a society if it is in the hands of one person, who uses it for his own benefit, or for that of a party ideal. All human dignity and freedom can be lost.

Everyone has met some kind of tyranny in his own life, and perhaps behaved that way himself. It is a method of government that can only work through fear.

This is a description of what can happen in a country where there is absolute dictatorship, with terrorist methods, used by secret police.

At midnight Rubashov, a high party official, wakes from his recurrent dream of being arrested and hears hammering on the door.

The two men who had come to arrest Rubashov stood outside on the dark landing and consulted each other. The porter, Vassilij, who had shown them the way upstairs, stood in the open lift doorway and panted with fear. He was a thin old man; above the torn collar of the military overcoat he had thrown over his night shirt appeared a broad red scar which gave him a scrofulous look . . .

It was cold, dark, and very quiet on the staircase. The younger of the two men from the Commissariat of the Interior proposed to shoot the lock of the door to pieces. Vassilij leant against the lift door; he had not had the time to put on his boots properly, and his hands trembled so much that he could not tie his laces. The elder of the two men was against shooting; the arrest had to be carried out discreetly. They both blew on their stiff hands and began again to hammer against the door; the younger banged on it with the butt of his revolver. A few floors below them a woman screamed in a piercing voice. 'Tell her to shut up,' said the young man to Vassilij. 'Be quiet,' shouted Vassilij. 'Here is authority.' The woman became quiet at once. The young man changed over to belabouring the door with his boots. The noise filled the whole staircase; at last the door fell open.

The three of them stood by Rubashov's bed, the young man with his pistol in his hand, the old man holding himself stiffly as though standing to attention; Vassilij stood a few steps behind them, leaning against the wall. Rubashov was still drying the sweat from the back of his head; he looked at them

short-sightedly with sleepy eyes. 'Citizen Rubashov
. . . we arrest you in the name of the law,' said the
young man. Rubashov felt for his glasses under the
pillow and propped himself up a bit. Now that he
had his glasses on, his eyes had the expression which
Vassilij and the other officials knew from old photographs and colour prints. The older official stood
more stiffly to attention; the young one, who had
grown up under new heroes, went a step closer to
the bed; all three saw that he was about to say or do
something brutal to hide his awkwardness.

'Put that gun away, comrade,' said Rubashov to
him. 'What do you want with me anyhow?'

'You hear you are arrested,' said the boy. 'Put
your clothes on and don't make a fuss.'

'Have you got a warrant?' asked Rubashov.

The elder official pulled a paper out of his
pocket, passed it to Rubashov and stood again to
attention.

Rubashov read it attentively. 'Well, good,' he
said. 'One is never any the wiser from those things;
the devil take you.'

'Put your clothes on and hurry up,' said the boy.
One saw that his brutality was no longer put on, but
was natural to him. A fine generation we have
produced, thought Rubashov. He recalled the
propaganda posters on which youth was always
represented with a laughing face. He felt very
tired. 'Pass me my dressing gown, instead of fumbling
about with your revolver,' he said to the boy. The
boy reddened but remained silent. The elder official
passed the dressing gown to Rubashov . . . They
watched him as he got slowly out of bed and collected
his crumpled clothes together.

The house was silent after the one shrill woman's
cry, but they had the feeling that all the inhabitants
were awake in their beds, holding their breath. Then
they heard someone in an upper storey pull the plug
and the water rushed down evenly through the pipes.

Arthur Koestler

Answer these questions:

1 How do people in the house react to these policemen?
2 What differences do you notice between the two men who come to arrest Rubashov?
3 Can you suggest any reasons why the younger man behaves as he does?
4 Look at Rubashov's comment on the warrant. What does this suggest about the system of justice?
5 Imagine someone in your neighbourhood being arrested in the middle of the night. How do you think the policeman or the neighbours might behave?

The danger that arises when authority is wrongly used is that it will be rejected altogether. This can mean revolution, which does not always succeed in changing things. Here is a list of some ways in which those in authority can see themselves. Have you noticed any others? Which do you feel is the ideal?

1 I know better than those under me and so do not need to consult them.
2 I should like to know the feelings and problems of those for whom I am responsible before I make decisions.
3 I see myself as a guide, not a dictator.

Most people get used to using authority themselves as they grow up. They learn from experience how order and happiness, or fear and chaos, can be the result of the actions of those in charge.

People depend on the authority of this policeman

These questions may help you to get authority into focus, for it is not as unreasonable or unnecessary as some people feel.

1 Have you ever been in authority, looked after younger children, helped to run a game, been a prefect?
2 What does it feel like? What problems does it raise? Do people treat you differently — are they more friendly or less friendly?
3 What is it like when you suddenly want to go free, feel an impulse to go wild, throw off restrictions and get away from authority?
4 When have you found authority to be most reassuring and helpful? When has it seemed at its worst?
5 Can people protest against bad authority without creating divisions and disorder?
6 Are there any areas where you feel more authority is needed in your own country or in the world? Why is the need for authority and respect important in areas like war and peace, advertising, family life?

There is usually conflict in a family as young people grow up.

Act a situation in which a boy or girl has a quarrel with parents. Is there a way to solve it?

You probably live in a democratic society. This means that when you are old enough you can vote for the people you feel will govern best. If you disagree with the party in power, you may want to try to make sure they know your point of view, and you might take part in protest demonstrations, organise petitions, write to the newspapers, or go out on strike.

This is the right of freedom of speech. Most governments will take notice of honest grievances and deal with them. They realise that true law and order can only exist under an authority that is accepted and respected, with which it is possible to co-operate. Force or pressure will normally lead to some kind of rebellion.

If you were in charge of the government, the school, the church or the town council, how would you make sure that you knew what people really want, and that it is good and right? How would you control troublemakers who just want to disturb the lives of others without real reason?

URGENT!
All members must attend the next meeting of the School Council on Friday

The Debate
on the RECENT PRICE RISES will be held next week
Make your views known to your M.P.

YOUR VOTE IS NEEDED!
AT THE NEXT COUNCIL MEETING, A VOTE WILL BE TAKEN ON THE GRANTING OF FUNDS FOR A NEW YOUTH CLUB. **Make sure you are there!**

A great danger is that authority will be used in a negative way, rather than to give a positive lead. 'Do not' can provoke the wrong reaction. Human beings always seem to be ready to do the opposite.

Perhaps this is one of the greatest changes Christ expected the Jews to make in their attitude to law. The Ten Commandments of Moses were right and good, but Christ expected more. He wanted the laws obeyed in a positive spirit of love.

The Commandments of Moses	Christ makes the Law perfect
1 Thou shalt love the Lord thy God and him only shalt thou serve.	You must worship God sincerely. Matthew 5, v. 23–24
2 Do not take the name of the Lord in vain.	There is no need to swear by anything. Matthew 5, v. 34–37
3 Keep holy the Sabbath day.	Remember the Sabbath is made for man. Mark 2, v. 27
4 Honour your parents.	Always put your duty to your parents first. Matthew 15, v. 4–7
5 Thou shalt not kill.	Always keep your temper. Matthew 5, v. 22
6 Thou shalt not commit adultery.	Forgive the adulterer but avoid the sin. John 8, v. 7–11
7 Thou shalt not steal.	We have all we need by the generosity of God. Matthew 6, v. 27–30
8 Thou shalt not bear false witness against thy neighbour.	Be merciful about your judgements. Matthew 7, v. 1–5

9 Thou shalt not covet thy neighbour's wife.	Be careful how you look at a woman or a man.
	Matthew 5, v. 27–28
10 Thou shalt not covet they neighbour's goods.	Set your heart on what really matters.
	Matthew 6, v. 19–20

10 Christian freedom

Authority and freedom can appear to conflict. How can someone be truly free if he or she has to obey someone else, for whatever reason? How can anyone be free if he is bound by laws and rules, with punishments to follow if they are disobeyed?

Or are we talking about real freedom?

What is freedom? Is it as elusive as the words of this song seem to suggest?

> Freedom come, Freedom go,
> Tell me 'Yes', then she tell me 'No!'
> Freedom never stay long,
> Freedom moving along.
> Freedom come, Freedom stay
> Freedom laugh and then she flies away
> Freedom never stay long
> Freedom moving along.

Make a list of things people would like to be free from, or free for.

e.g. free from hunger, want, hatred . . .

free for laughter, love, sharing . . .

Freedom is surely more than a feeling that you should have nothing to bother you.

The following story is called *Freedom to Love*. Is the situation familiar to you?

It was fifteen below zero one evening, when, just at dusk, Johnny Hall and I climbed into his open sleigh

and started out for White Harbour, thirty-five miles and ten hours away . . .

During the last two hours both of us, I think, were a little delirious from the cold. I cursed the day when I had taken up the study of medicine. I thought of all the other occupations in which a man could engage, in which the hours were regular, and he could work in comfortable surroundings, and be warm all the time. I remember having bitter thoughts, too, about the patient we were going to see. He was probably sitting up at this very moment alongside a hot stove, drinking rum and hot water and laughing to himself at how he was making a fool of the new doctor. He would, of course, not pay me — almost no one ever did on these trips, even though they might have the money cached in a tin box under the bed — but would promise to pay when his cheque came in. Everyone, I had already found, was always expecting a cheque from somewhere or other soon. It was this imaginary currency that I was paid with nine-tenths of the time. The real dollars were kept for more important uses than paying the doctor. All of a sudden, with all my heart, I hated this patient I had never seen. I hated the country and I hated my own profession most of all.

Finally we arrived at the small house where the patient lay. As soon as I saw him, I forgot all about hating him. He was a very sick man, and he was in extreme pain. I knew what was wrong with him before I got near the bed and before I heard a word of his story.

The operation, although it involves a three-inch incision through the lower part of the abdomen, is a simple one and it did not take long to do. The transformation in the patient was something to see. He actually cried with relief and joy, and in a little while, he was sleeping the quiet sleep of exhaustion.

The woman gave me another cup of hot tea. As I drank it and smoked a cigarette I thought, 'So what if I get paid with an imaginary cheque, and if I have to pay Johnny Hall with real and not imaginary dollars, and if there are lots of comfortable easy jobs with regular hours! This is worth doing!'

The message of this story is surely that freedom becomes a reality when it has been earned, when you have freed yourself in a conflict from the temptation to be purely selfish. You have proved you are free to act as you really believe you should act – and so have become more truly yourself.

The following story sums up some of the conflicts that people experience in coming to terms with the problems of getting a true view of themselves and the world in which they live. It is from a novel set in Russia in the last century, but the genius of the author makes it fresh and real for us to think about today.

But she could not love as truly as I did because she was frigid and already sufficiently corrupted. Already there was a demon in her who whispered day and night that she was a ravishing, divine creature, and she, who had no idea what she had been created for and for what purpose life had been given her, imagined herself in the future as rich and as moving in the highest aristocratic circles. She dreamed of balls, races, liveries, sumptuous drawing-rooms, her own salon, and a whole swarm of counts, princes, ambassadors, famous painters and actors, all of them adoring her and admiring her beauty and her dresses . . . This craving for personal power and personal success, and this continual concentration of all one's thoughts in one direction, dampens people's ardour, and Ariadne was cold – to me, to nature, and to music. Meanwhile time was passing and still there were no ambassadors in sight. Ariadne went on living with her brother, the spiritualist;

things went from bad to worse, till in the end she had no money to buy hats or dresses with and she had to resort to all kinds of tricks and stratagems to conceal her poverty.

As luck would have it a certain Prince Maktuyev, a wealthy but utterly worthless man, had proposed to her when she was living at her aunt's in Moscow. She had refused him point blank. But now she was sometimes tortured by a growing sense of regret. Why had she refused him? Just as a peasant blows with disgust on a mug of kvass with cockroaches floating about in it and yet drinks it, so she frowned disdainfully at the recollection of the Prince and yet would say to me: 'Say what you like but there is something inexplicable, something fascinating about a title!'

She dreamed of a title, of cutting a great figure in high society, but at the same time she did not want to let me slip through her fingers. However you may dream of ambassadors, your heart is not a stone and you can't help being indulgent towards your own youth. Ariadne tried hard to fall in love, she pretended to, she even swore she loved me. But I am a nervous and extremely sensitive man; when I am loved, I can feel it even at a distance, without vows and assurances, but with Ariadne I immediately felt a coldness in the air, and when she talked to me of love I seemed to be listening to the singing of a nightingale made of metal. Ariadne herself felt that she was lacking in conviction. She was vexed and more than once I saw her burst into tears. Why, one evening on the riverbank she flung her arms round me impulsively and kissed me, but I could see from her eyes that she did not love me, that she had embraced me merely out of curiosity, to test herself, to see what came of it. And I was horrified. I took her hand and cried in despair,

'Those caresses without love make me unhappy'.

'What a strange fellow you are!' she said with vexation, and walked away.   Anton Chekhov

Things to think about

1 Is it likely that Ariadne would be happy? If not, why not?

2 Is there any way that the hero of the story could show Ariadne that the one thing that really matters is being able to love others?

3 Why do you think that Ariadne is really selfish? How is she making herself a prisoner of what she wants so that she misses a good deal of other things that are very valuable to her?

4 What lesson does this passage have for a Christian about the need for Christ in the world?

5 It is not wrong to have ambitions to better yourself. But Ariadne has not learnt that it is people who matter. What should she know about the real purpose of life, 'what she has been created for'?

So what is freedom?

As with other vitally important issues in human life, it is most perfectly expressed in Christ's own life.

It is not the avoidance of danger and difficulty but the acceptance of it as a challenge which is in some way an expression of our true strength and potential as human beings, with the power to choose and endure for the sake of truth, and love, and justice.

The life of Christ has inspired countless others to suffer and even die to gain freedom for others. It is something that grows and widens as people learn to live unselfishly.

Make a list of the things people might do if they could act just as they wished. Write beside it the consideration that might prevent them doing it:

e.g.

| Say what they felt like saying to a teacher. | The teacher may have been right in the criticism made. |

Sometimes it is fear that prevents an evil action. Terrible punishments have been used in the past — a thief's hand could be cut off; an adultress could be stoned.

These are deterrents, but they do not provide a guarantee that people are free to live as they should. Sometimes it seems that sin begets more sin, and no one can really break free for a second chance.

The whole message of Christianity is that we are set free to live a truly human life because of Jesus Christ's sacrifice. How can more people learn to understand and live in joy because of this truth? Does it truly have the potential to change the world? Everyone has to choose to accept or reject Christ and the freedom he offers.

> For this reason we always pray for you, ever since we heard about you. We ask God to fill you with the knowledge of his will, with all the wisdom and understanding that his Spirit gives. Then you will be able to live as the Lord wants, and always do what pleases him. Your lives will be fruitful in all kinds of good works, and you will grow in your knowledge of God. May you be made strong with all the strength which comes from his glorious might, so that you may be able to endure everything with patience. And give thanks, with joy, to the Father, who has made you fit to have your share of what God has reserved for his people in the kingdom of light. He rescued us from the power of darkness and brought us safe into the kingdom of his dear Son, by whom we are set free, that is, our sins are forgiven.
>
> Colossians 1, v. 9–14

Appendix

Bible Service

Members of the class should be chosen to lead the prayers or
do the readings:

Opening Hymn   To be chosen from those available.

Opening Prayer   Lord,
the edges of my mind
and the shape of my world
are as fuzzy as the night mist.

I'm not sure where I am, often,
where I am going,
why I think the thoughts I do
and whether it's worth
searching for something.

It's like being in a daze
without any sense of direction
or clear road ahead.

It's like wrestling with the sand
. . . in an endless desert.

Is there some old angel in the woods
who can grab me by the throat,
and twist my wandering mind
until I feel the real,
taste the true,
wonder at the world
and get a glimpse
of where to go tomorrow?

Would you take me on, Lord,
show me the nerves of nature

and shock me into my senses
until I feel the way?
Or will you just shine on trees
and forget about me?

Well, I won't let you go
until you bless me,
bless me with the instinct of a bird
who knows who he is
and which way to fly
when it is winter.
I won't let you go,
I won't!

The First Reading is from the Letter of St Paul to the Romans
Romans 6, v. 15, 16, 20–22

Prayers and Response

Response   May we use your freedom well, Lord.

Prayers   I   We pray that we may never do any-
                          thing that destroys our freedom or
                          that of someone else.

                  II   We pray that no one may be led into
                          sinful ways through our influence

                  III   We pray that each human being may
                          be given the opportunity to enjoy their
                          freedom to live as God intends them to
                          live, in dignity and peace.

                  IV   We pray that each word, thought and
                          action of ours may be under our
                          control, to be directed as you wish,
                          in love.

The Second Reading is from the Letter of St Paul to the Ephesians
Ephesians 1, v. 3–10

Closing Prayer Our Father . . .

Closing Hymn 'We Shall Overcome', or any suitable hymn.